MARIECHEN DANZ

CUBE CELL STAGE

DISTANZ

Cover:
Rhyme and Reason (detail), Performance, 24 May 2012,
GAK Gesellschaft für Aktuelle Kunst Bremen.

GESELLSCHAFT FÜR AKTUELLE KUNST BREMEN

KUNSTVEREIN GÖTTINGEN

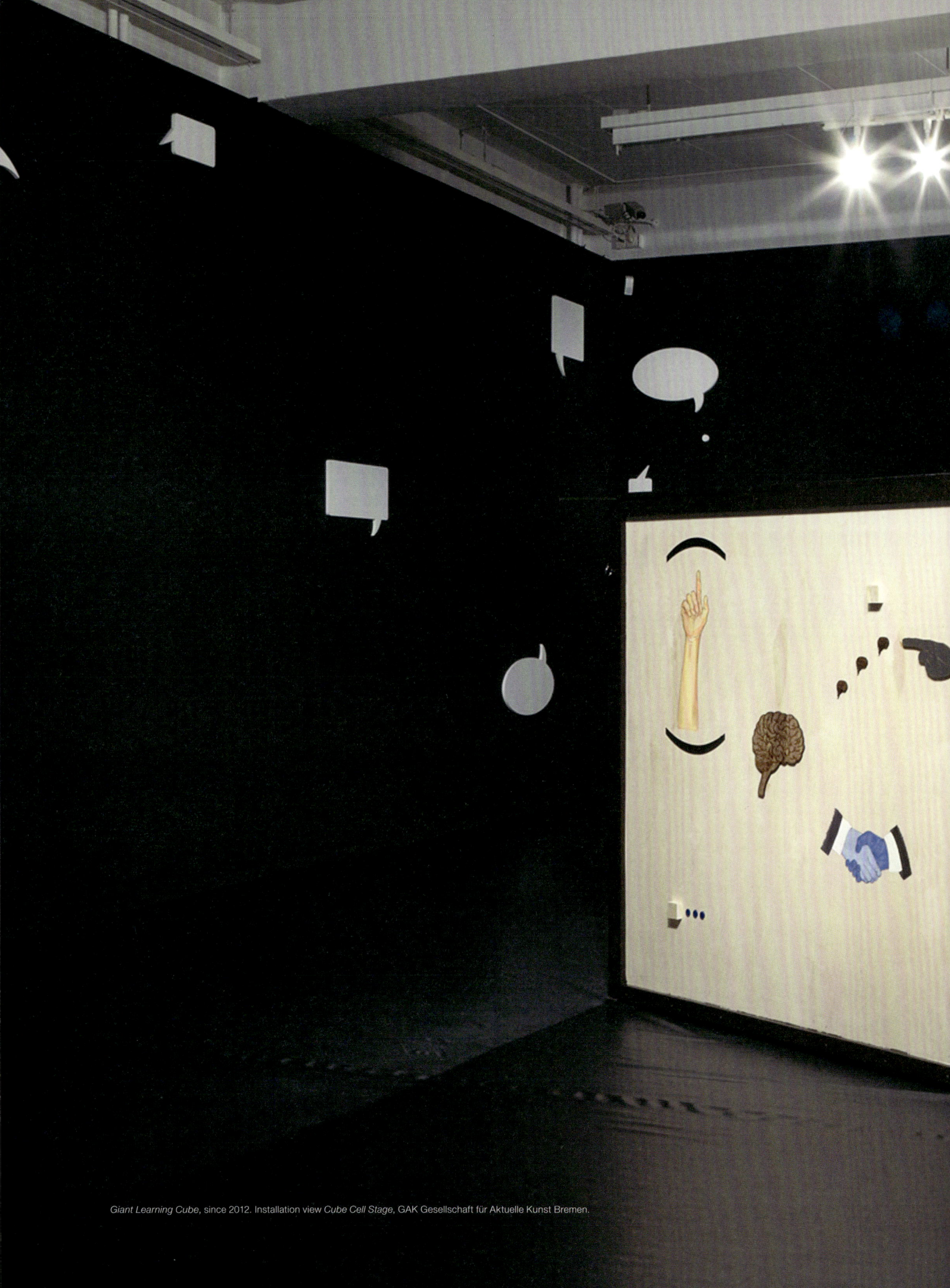

Giant Learning Cube, since 2012. Installation view *Cube Cell Stage*, GAK Gesellschaft für Aktuelle Kunst Bremen.

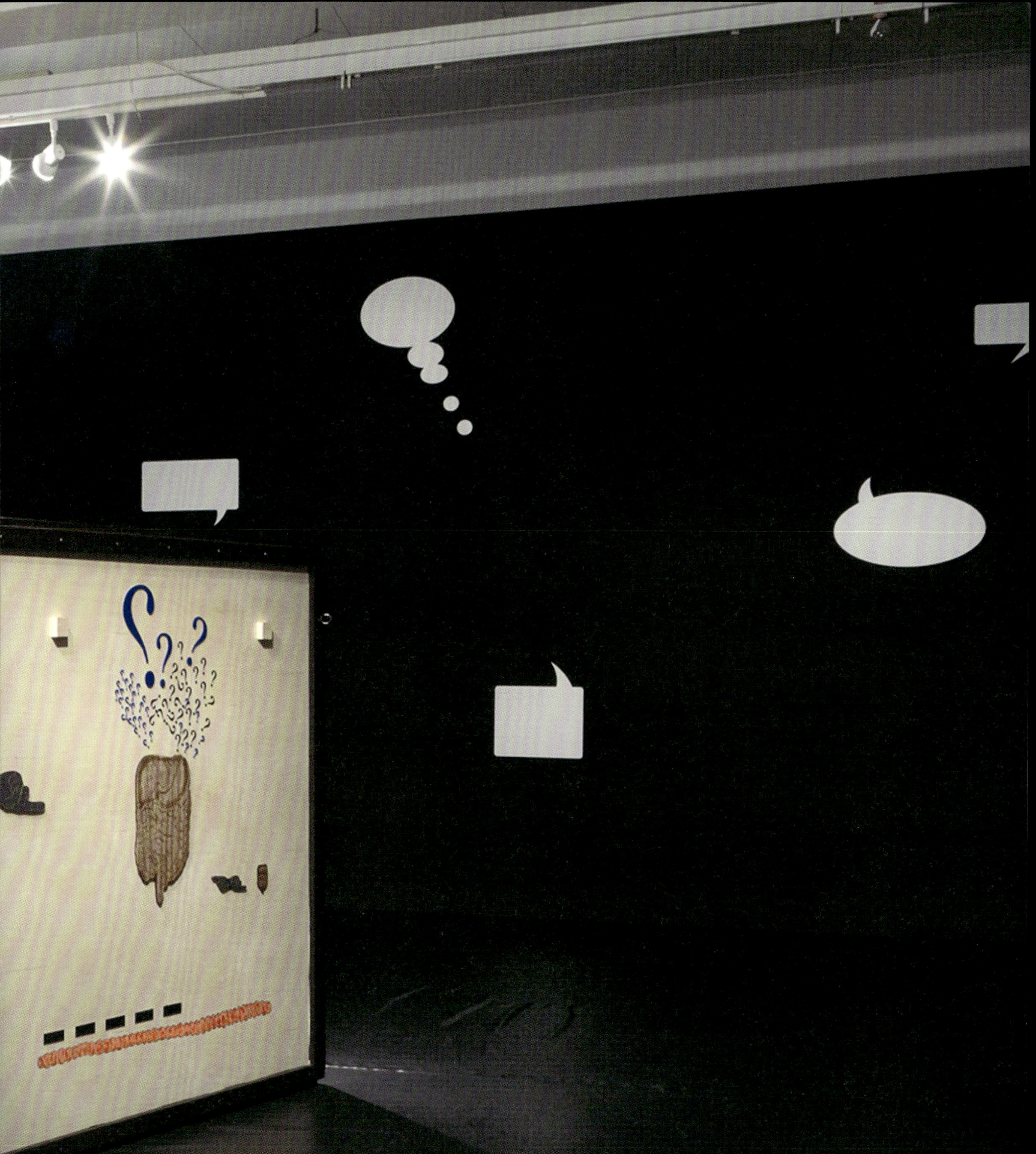

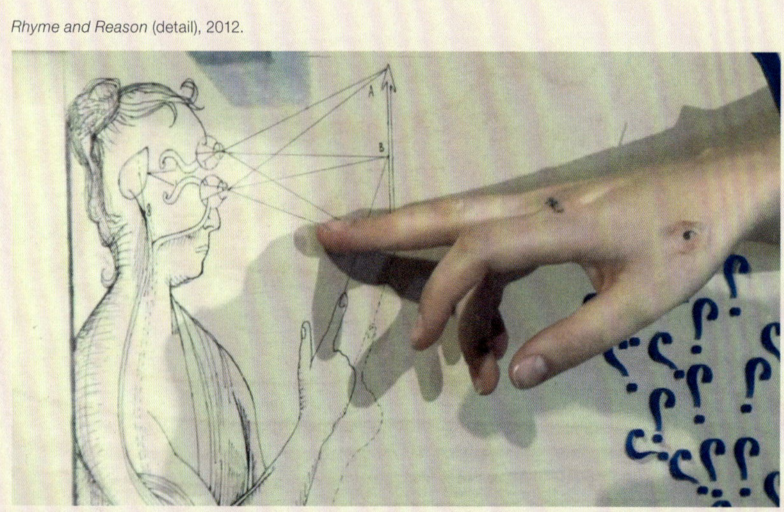

Rhyme and Reason (detail), 2012.

INHALT CONTENTS

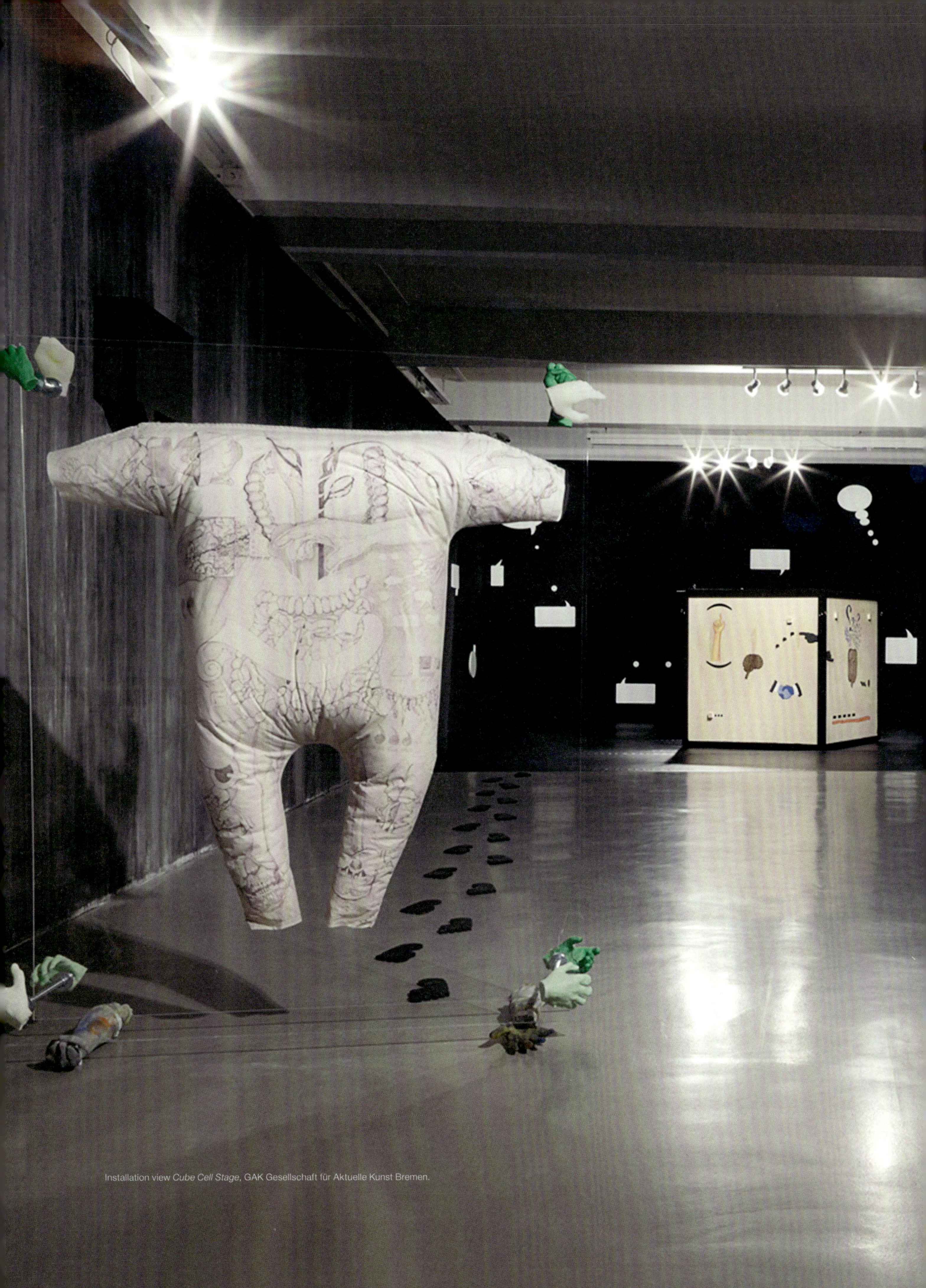

Installation view *Cube Cell Stage*, GAK Gesellschaft für Aktuelle Kunst Bremen.

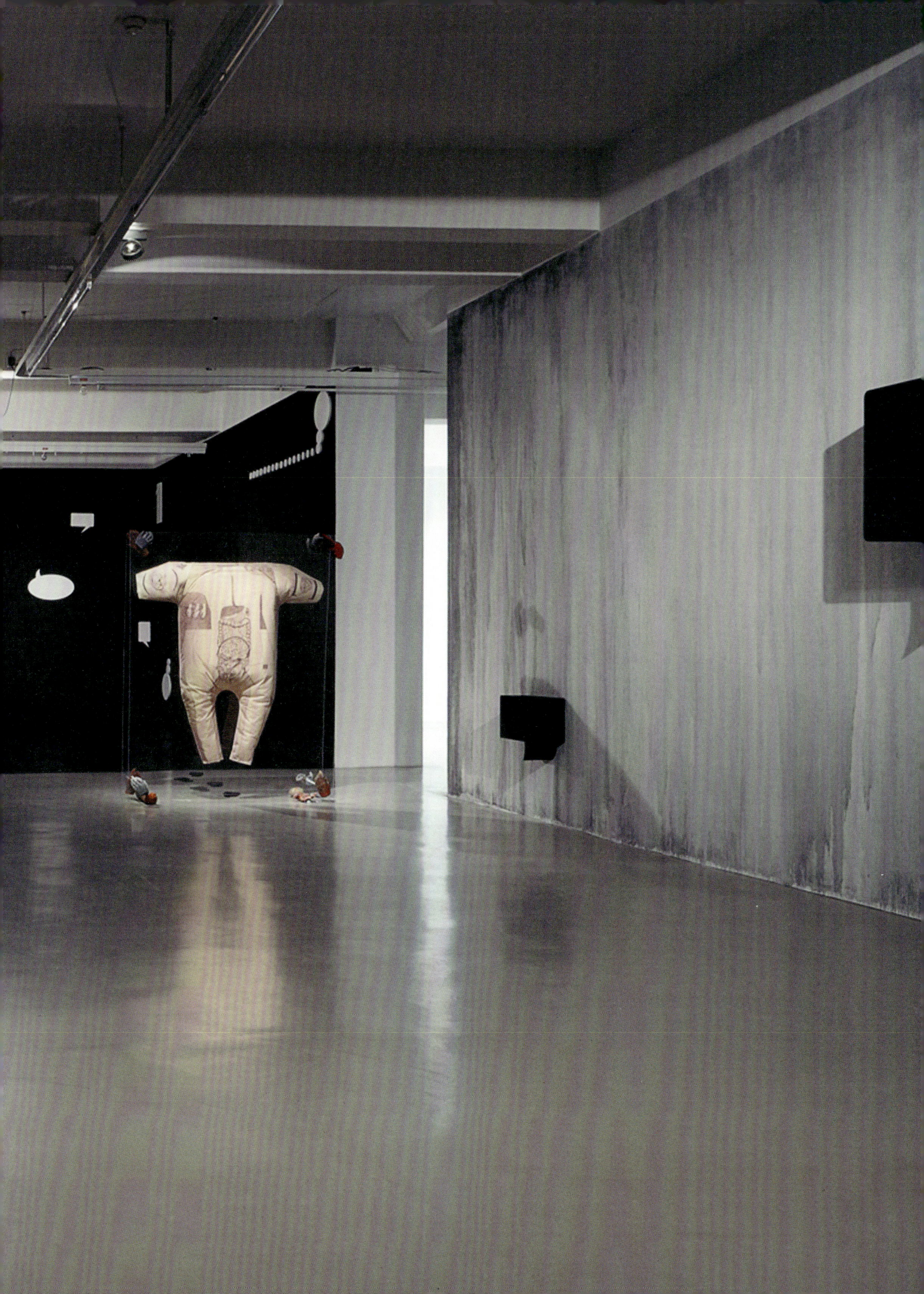

„WHERE ALL THE TROUBLE COMES FROM“[1]

JANNEKE DE VRIES

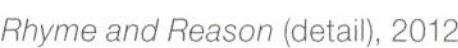

Rhyme and Reason (detail), 2012.

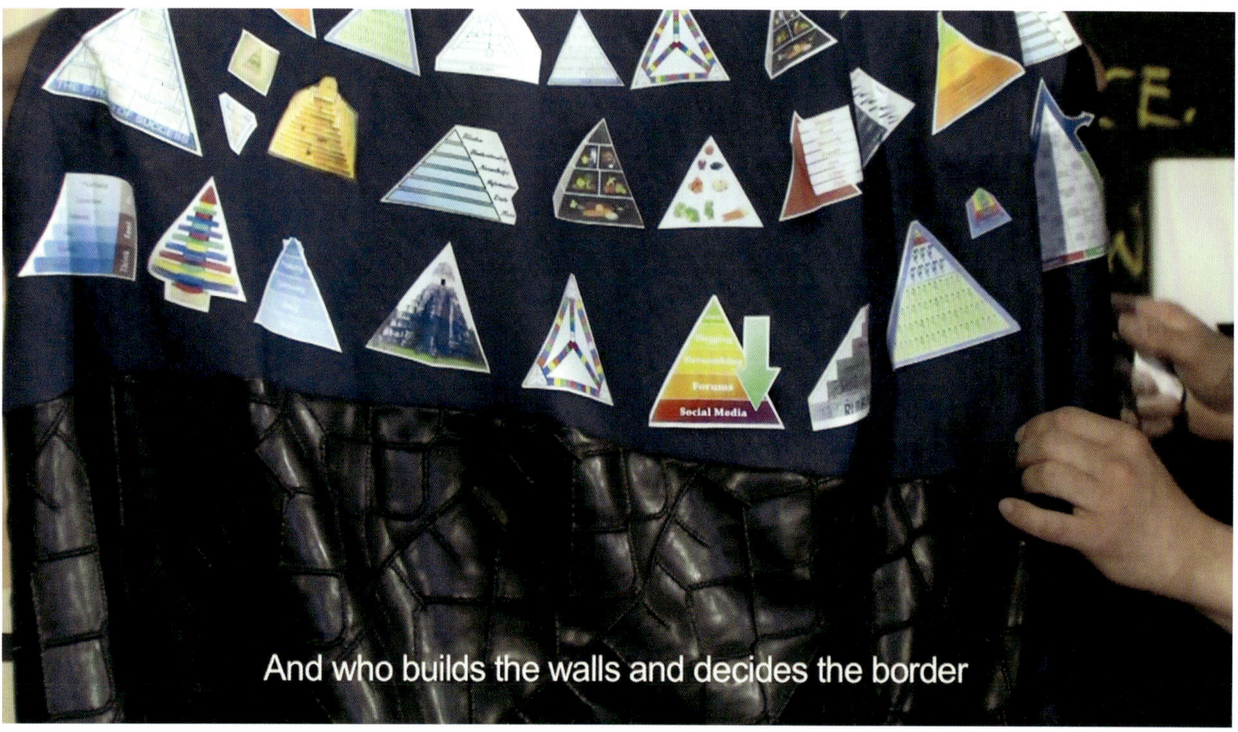

Das künstlerische Schaffen von Mariechen Danz mag einem zunächst wie ein unentwirrbares Knäuel von Techniken, Materialien, Formen und Gedanken erscheinen. Meint man einmal, einen Faden entwirrt zu haben, entpuppt er sich meist schnell als Verbindungsknoten zu gleich mehreren anderen, lässt sich nicht lösen und zieht einen immer tiefer hinein in den Kosmos der Künstlerin. Ihr Denken verortet sich zwischen den Gegensatzpaaren von Körper und Verstand, Objektivität und Subjektivität, Wissenschaft und kindlichen Lernprozessen, Gegenwart und Geschichte, kollektivem Wissen und persönlicher Erfahrung, Spontanität und Kalkül sowie Hochkultur und Pop. Es ist an manchen Stellen überbordend und geradezu rauschhaft, um an anderen wieder minimalistisch kühl zu argumentieren. Und es bezieht die Möglichkeit des Versagens oder Missverständnisses ausdrücklich mit ein. Dieses Vorgehen ist Programm und entspringt der klar getroffenen Entscheidung, dass alles wert ist, berücksichtigt zu werden, weil nichts allein eine Lösung bieten kann. Mariechen Danz hinterfragt die Kategorien, in denen sich unsere eurozentristischen Geschichtsbilder bewegen, die Art und Weise, wie Wissen überliefert und (meist ohne zu hinterfragen) übernommen wird – kurz, sie sucht, die Schubladen wieder zu öffnen und durcheinander zu bringen, in die wir unsere Welt zur besseren Überschaubarkeit einteilen. Sie glaubt nicht an die Methoden, die wir uns im Laufe der Zeit zurechtgelegt haben, um Informationen aufzunehmen und zu kommunizieren. Vielmehr geht es ihr darum, gleichwertig und vergleichend nebeneinander zu stellen, auch vergangene oder abgelehnte Wege einzubeziehen und ein Bewusstsein dafür zu schaffen, dass die Dinge immer auch anders sein könnten, als wir sie zu wissen meinen, und wir in dem Moment, wo wir uns für eine Sichtweise entscheiden, etwas anderes ausschließen.

Eine unkritische Annahme des Vorgegebenen unterwirft sich dagegen den hierarchischen Strukturen, die jedem Wissen, jeder Entscheidung und nahezu jeder Kommunikation innewohnen. Und sie bestätigt eine Form von irreführender Objektivität. Denn irgendwann hat irgendwer irgendwo entschieden und weitergegeben, was richtig und was falsch ist – ein zutiefst subjektives, exkludierendes und machtorientiertes Vorgehen. Es wundert demnach nicht, dass Mariechen Danz formal wie inhaltlich immer wieder auf kultur- und sozialanthropologische Aspekte der Postkolonialismusdebatte zurückgreift und sich dabei vor allem auf das Deterritorialisierungskonzept von Félix Guattari und Gilles Deleuze bezieht. Deleuze und Guattari verknüpfen seit Anfang der 1970er Jahre die Geschichte und Funktionsweisen von Macht und Wissen existenziell mit territorialen und damit hierarchischen Fragen[2] – beinhaltet z.B. der landläufige Ablauf in der Kolonialisierungsgeschichte, dass sich ein Volk einem anderen subjektiv überlegen fühlte,

The work of Mariechen Danz may initially appear a tangle of techniques, materials, forms, and ideas that are evidently impossible to unravel. Just when one thinks one has managed to unsnarl one thread, it turns out to be knotted to a web of others and refuses to come undone, leading ever deeper into the cosmos of the artist. Danz' thinking is poised between the opposites of body and mind, objectivity and subjectivity, science and childhood learning processes, present and history, collective knowledge and personal experience, spontaneity and strategic calculation, high culture and pop. In some instances it is exuberant or even ecstatic; in others it assumes a cool, minimalistic line of argumentation. And it explicitly incorporates the potential for failure or misunderstanding. This approach is programmatic of her work and based on a conscious decision to view everything as worthy of consideration, because nothing can offer a solution by itself. Mariechen Danz questions the categories that dictate our Eurocentric notions of history and the way knowledge is transmitted and passed on (usually without being questioned). In short, she attempts to open up and jumble the compartments into which we have neatly divided the world in order to make it more manageable. She does not believe in the methods that we have established over time to process information and to communicate. Instead, she is interested in placing things on an equal level, comparing them, incorporating past or rejected paths and creating a consciousness for the fact that the things we believe to know can always be different in actuality and that in the moment of deciding to assume a certain perspective, we exclude others.

An approach of noncritical acceptance is, however, subject to the hierarchical structures that are inherent to any form of knowledge, any decision, and almost any type of communication. And it simply affirms a form of deceptive objectivity. Because at some point someone somewhere decided what was right and what was wrong and passed this on—a deeply subjective, exclusive and power-oriented process. It is no wonder that Danz consistently draws on cultural and socio-anthropological elements of the postcolonial debate, both formally and in terms of content. The deterritorialization concept of Félix Guattari and Gilles Deleuze serves as one of her primary sources of reference in this context. From the early 1970s onwards Deleuze and Guattari explored the existential link between the history and mechanisms of power and territorial and hierarchical issues.[2] For example, this addresses how over the course of the long history of colonialization one people subjectively felt superior to another, taking the other's territory, exploiting the other economically, and imposing its culture. The idea of deterritorialization attempts to dissolve

deren Territorium übernahm, es ökonomisch aussaugte und im Gegenzug seine Kultur aufzwang. Dieses Denken sucht die Deterritorialisierung im Sinne einer Gleichwertigkeit aufzulösen mittels der „Trennung sozialer, politischer oder kultureller Praktiken von ihren Ursprungsorten und –völkern“[3]. Dass es im Zuge einer solchen Neuordnung zwangsläufig wieder zu einer Form der Territorialisierung kommt, ist Bestandteil des Diskurses. Doch Voraussetzung dieser „Reterritorialisierung“ ist zunächst die Öffnung der gegebenen Systeme und der mit ihnen verbundenen Machtverteilungen: Die Karten werden neu gemischt, ein verändertes Denken wird möglich. Es ist genau diese Idee, die das künstlerische Schaffen von Mariechen Danz antreibt.

In ihrer Infragestellung gängiger Konzepte ist sich Danz auch der historischen Irrtümer der Geschichtsschreibung bewusst: Einstein z. B. war ein guter Schüler. Nicht Charles Lindbergh überflog als Erster den Atlantik, sondern John Alcock und Arthur Whitten Brown im Jahr 1919 (als Lindbergh 1927 das Meer im Flugzeug überquerte, hatten das bereits 66 Personen vor ihm getan). Und die Annahme, die Erde sei eine Scheibe, hat es so nicht gegeben. Bereits in der Antike kam man zu dem Schluss, sie müsse eine Kugel sein. Selbst der Fehler ein Fehler also... Diese Liste falscher Lesarten der Historie ließe sich beliebig fortführen. In der Statistik – der Wissenschaft, die ganz besonders einer Form von Objektivität verpflichtet scheint – hat die Erkenntnis, dass systematische Fehler und damit ein Einbruch subjektiver Momente unvermeidbar sind, dazu geführt, dass man sie nicht nur als Größe mit einberechnet, sondern ihnen auch einen Namen gegeben hat: Bias (engl. „Verzerrung“). In die Arbeit von Mariechen Danz finden vor allem die Fehler der Medizin und Anatomie Eingang. Eines der bekanntesten Beispiele ist dabei sicher Galen von Pergamon (129–199 n. Chr.). Als berühmtester Arzt der Antike legte er die Grundlagen der anatomischen Beschaffenheit des menschlichen Körpers bis in die Renaissance hinein fest, ohne dass sie von Dritten überprüft oder auch nur in Frage gestellt worden wären. Viele von Galens Ansichten waren jedoch falsch, da er seine Sektionen an Schweinen, Affen und Hunden durchführte und die so gewonnenen Erkenntnisse auf den Menschen übertrug. Erst Andreas Vesalius erkannte im 16. Jahrhundert, dass Galen wohl nie einen Menschen seziert hatte.[4]

Sehr unmittelbar bezieht sich die Künstlerin in ihrer Produktion auf den Beginn aller Wissenskommunikation. So integriert sie etwa frühe Lernwerkzeuge von Kindern wie die allbekannten ABC-Würfel sowie Hängekarten und Schreibtafeln aus der Schule (der Ort, an dem die Koexistenz von Wissen und Nicht-Wissen allgegenwärtig ist, wie wir alle erfahren mussten). In dieser Erkenntnis, dass eben nicht nur der Fehler,

this kind of thinking in favor of a more balanced approach through the “severance of social, political, or cultural practices from their native places and populations.”[3] That a new form of territorialization occurs within this process of realignment is part of the discourse. However, the basis of such a “reterritorialization” is first the opening of the given system and its associated distribution of power: The cards are reshuffled, and a new form of thinking becomes possible. It is this very idea that the work of Mariechen Danz puts into artistic practice.

In questioning established concepts Danz is also aware of the errors that have been written into history. For example, Einstein was a good student. Charles Lindbergh was not the first to fly over the Atlantic; the first flights were conducted by John Alcock and Arthur Whitten Brown in 1919 (when Lindbergh crossed the ocean in his plane in 1927, 66 people had already done so before him). And the assumption that the earth was flat had not existed as such. Already in antiquity the conclusion was drawn that the earth must be round. Even the mistake was a mistake... This list of the false readings of history could be continued ad infinitum. In statistics—a science that is evidently highly indebted to a mode of objectivity—it is generally understood that systematic mistakes and thus also the interference of subjective elements are unavoidable; this had led to them not only being calculated as a variable but they have also been given a name: “bias.” Danz’ works particularly incorporate mistakes from the fields of medicine and anatomy. One of the most popular of such examples is certainly the work of Galen of Pergamon (129–199 A.D.). As a famous doctor of antiquity he laid the foundations of the anatomical make-up of the human body, which persisted well into the Renaissance without being reappraised or questioned by another party. But many of Galen’s notions were incorrect, since he performed his sections on pigs, monkeys, and dogs, applying then what he had learned to the human body. Only in the 16th century did Andreas Vesalius realize that Galen had never dissected a human body.[4]

In her practice Danz makes immediate references to the very beginnings of the communication of knowledge. She thus integrates early learning tools for children, such as the well known ABC cubes as well as classroom maps and chalkboards (suggesting the school as a place where the coexistence of knowing and not-knowing is omnipresent, as we have all experienced). Through the realization that not only mistakes but also knowledge lurk everywhere, Danz goes beyond the classical divisions of high and low culture: An additional and extremely important element of her artistic practice is her recourse to the strategies of the pop song, which serves as a perfect means of communicating content due to the accessibility of the format.

sondern ebenso das Wissen überall lauern kann, setzt sich Danz auch über die klassischen Einteilungen von high and low culture hinweg: Ein weiteres, sehr wesentliches Element ihrer künstlerischen Praxis ist etwa der Rückgriff auf die Strategien des Popsongs, der ihr in seiner Zugänglichkeit ein perfektes Mittel ist, um Inhalte zu kommunizieren.

Und so kreist das künstlerische Denken von Mariechen Danz wesentlich um folgende Fragen: Wer trifft die Entscheidungen, was etabliert, was in den Hintergrund verbannt und was wie weitergegeben wird? Gibt es eine Möglichkeit, das, was vergessen scheint, aber über Jahrhunderte sinnvoll genutzt wurde, in seinen Stärken wieder zu berücksichtigen – nicht im Sinne einer Wiederbelebung, sondern auf der Suche nach einer erfolgreichen Form der Kommunikation? Warum haben sich dagegen ausgerechnet die 26 lateinischen Buchstaben in unserem Kulturkreis durchgesetzt? Was wäre als Alternative zu dem denkbar, das wir als gesichert akzeptieren? Auf der Suche nach dem geringsten Ausschluss ist es deshalb nur konsequent, wenn Danz in ihrem eigenen Schaffen keiner Ausdrucksweise den Vorrang vor einer anderen einräumt, sondern sich in allen Gattungen äußert, die sich denken lassen – Zeichnung und Skulptur, Performance und Installation, Video und Gesang, Malerei und Fotografie. Auch dass sie ihre Arbeit meist in einen Prozess einbettet, der sich stückweise immer weiter entwickelt, entspringt ihrem Ringen um eine größtmögliche Offenheit, die sich Hierarchien bewusst macht, sich ihnen, so weit das überhaupt möglich ist, verweigert und strukturell flexibel bleibt.

Das Ausstellungsprojekt *Cube Cell Stage* führte die Gleichwertigkeit der Medien, Quellen und Gedanken sowie die Prozesshaftigkeit ihrer Arbeit exemplarisch vor: Es nahm seinen Anfang in der GAK Gesellschaft für Aktuelle Kunst in Bremen, fand dort mit der Performance *Rhyme and Reason* einen vorläufigen Höhepunkt und Abschluss, wurde kurze Zeit später im Kunstverein Göttingen verändert weitergeführt und begleitet die Künstlerin in Gestalt des sich kontinuierlich entwickelnden *Giant Learning Cube* bis heute. Diese Arbeit – ein großer Holzkubus mit vielfältig bemalten Seiten, der die kindlichen Lernwerkzeuge der ABC-Würfel monumentalisiert – bildete das Hauptelement der beiden Versionen von *Cube Cell Stage*. Er vereint alles, was der Ausstellungstitel anspricht: Zunächst ist er offensichtlicher „cube", sowohl in seiner äußeren Erscheinung als großer Würfel als auch in seiner Funktion, Träger künstlerischer Darstellungen innerhalb einer Ausstellungsinstitution und damit Anknüpfungspunkt für kunstimmanente Diskussionen um institutionelle Präsentation und Inszenierung zu sein.[5] Er ist übersät mit Bildern des menschlichen

Thus Mariechen Danz' artistic thinking largely centers on the following questions: Who decides what becomes established, what is banned to the shadows, and what is passed on? Is there a possibility of once again making room for the strengths of something that seems long forgotten but has been used meaningfully for centuries—not in the sense of a revival but by incorporating it into the search for a successful form of communication? Why, in contrast, have specifically 26 Latin letters become accepted in our cultural sphere? What are alternatives to the things that we have come to accept as certain? In her exploration of even the smallest exclusions, it is logical that Danz does not give precedence to one form of expression over others in her own artistic practice—drawing and sculpture, performance and installation, video and song, painting and photography. Also that her work is embedded in an ongoing, step by step process is owed to her struggle to achieve the greatest possible sense of openness, which creates an awareness of hierarchies, rejects them, to whatever extent possible, and offers structural flexibility.

The exhibition project *Cube Cell Stage* has been exemplary for the balance of media, sources, and ideas in Danz' work as well as its process-based nature. It began at the GAK Gesellschaft für Aktuelle Kunst in Bremen and came to an initial high point and conclusion with the performance *Rhyme and Reason*. Soon after it was developed further at Kunstverein Göttingen in a different form and still continues to accompany the artist today in the *Giant Learning Cube*, a work that is still developing and ongoing. A large wooden cube with varying painted sides that recalls the learning tool of a monumentalized ABC cube, it forms the main component of both versions of *Cube Cell Stage*. It brings together everything entailed in the exhibition title: It is obviously a "cube," both in its appearance and in its function as a carrier of artistic representations within an exhibition situation and thus also a point of contact for the discourses of art surrounding institutional presentation and staging.[5] It is strewn with images of the human body, punctuation marks and letters—stand-ins for the "cells," the nuclei of Mariechen Danz' artistic production, which are then taken a step further as "cell stage," referring to biological life cycles and thus also developmental processes, to which *Cube Cell Stage* is so indebted. And finally the cube is not only at the center of a situation recalling a theatrical drama, but the object itself also becomes a "stage" as soon as its sides are folded down. Since the end of the Göttingen exhibition, the *Giant Learning Cube* has been in a perpetual state of change, in which Danz has been adding anatomical illustrations and written elements to its walls and presenting the work in various new exhibition contexts.[6]

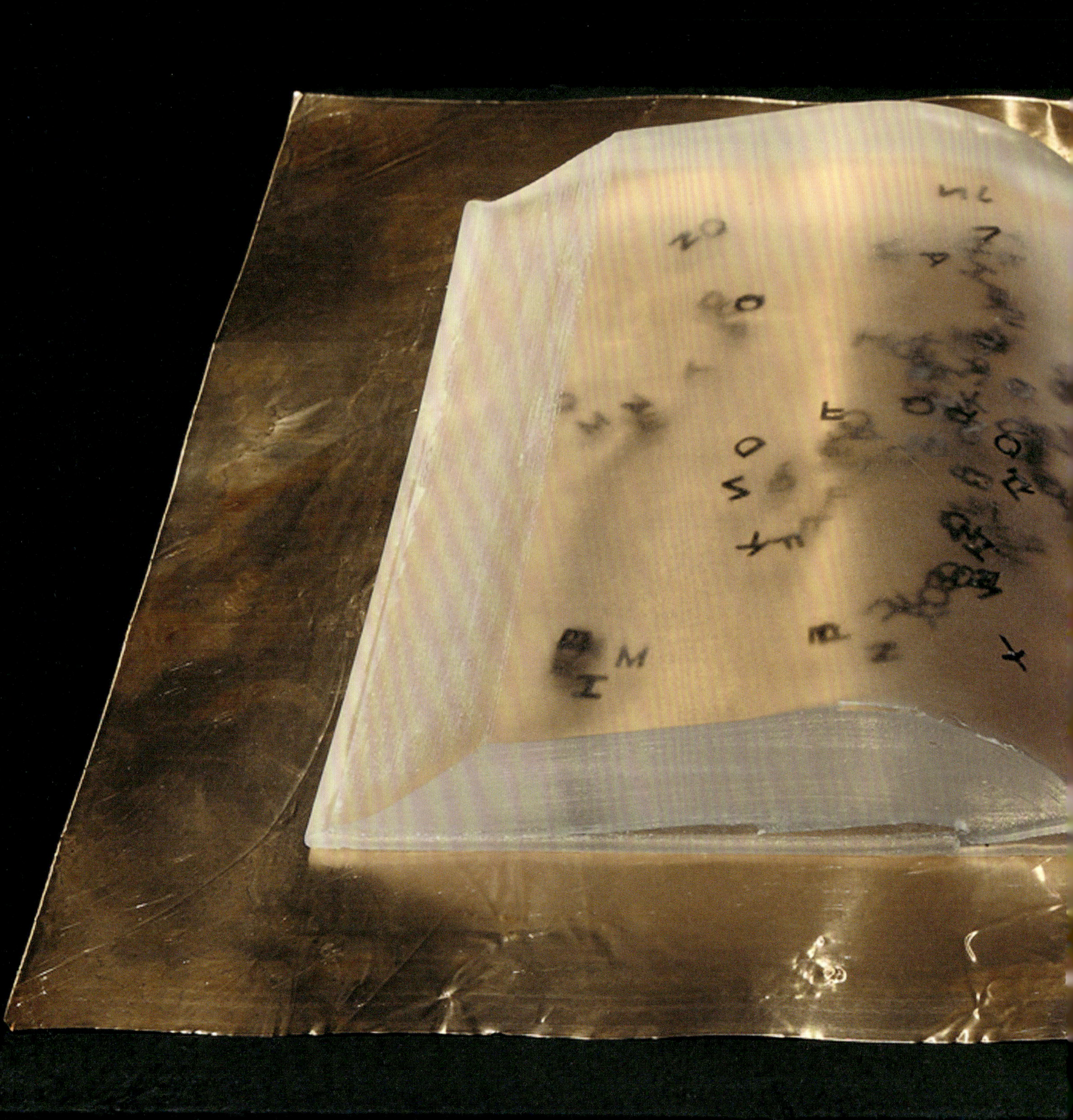

Book (unlearning) 1, 2012.

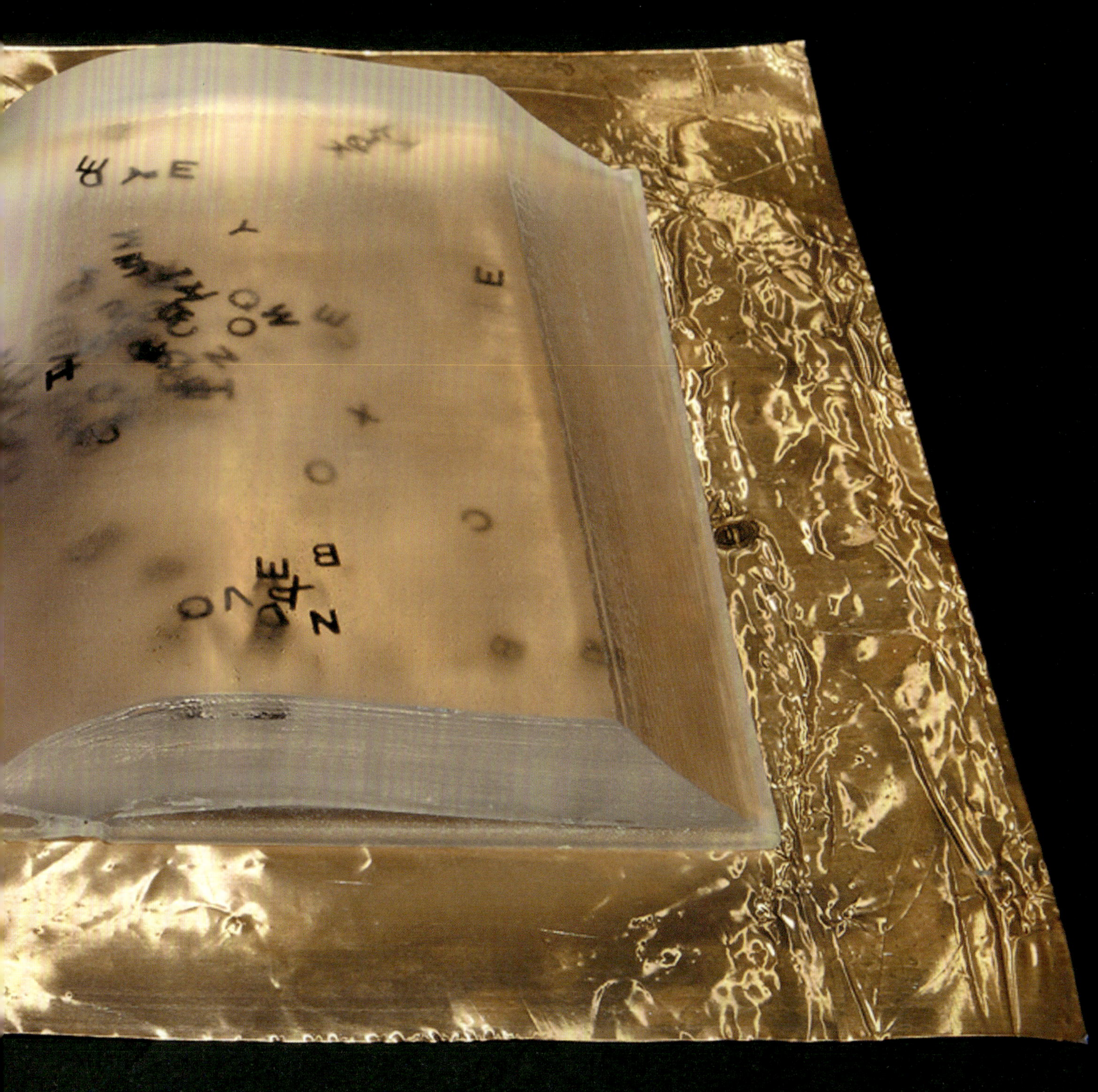

Körpers, mit Satzzeichen und Buchstaben – Stellvertretern für die „cells", die Keimzellen von Mariechen Danz' künstlerischer Produktion, die weitergedacht als „cell stage" auf biologische Zyklen und damit auf die Prozesshaftigkeit hinweisen, der *Cube Cell Stage* so wesentlich verpflichtet war. Und schließlich befindet der Würfel sich nicht nur inmitten einer bühnenhaft dramatisierten Situation, sondern ist selber Bühne – wird er doch vom „cube" zum „stage", sobald seine Seiten heruntergeklappt sind. Der *Giant Learning Cube* ist auch nach Beendigung der Göttinger Ausstellung in ständigem Wandel begriffen, indem Danz seine Wände in einem fortlaufenden Prozess mit anatomischen Darstellungen und Sprachelementen vervollständigt und ihn in unterschiedliche, neue Ausstellungskontexte integriert.[6]

Beide Versionen von *Cube Cell Stage*, sowohl in der GAK als auch im Kunstverein, basierten in besonderer Weise auf den Fragen nach dem WIE des Wissens: „How to know?", singt Danz in einem ihrer Songs, den sie auch in *Rhyme and Reason* integrierte.[7] WIE entsteht Wissen? WIE wird es kommuniziert und angeeignet? WIE kann man wissen, was faktisch richtig und falsch ist? Und WIE kann man diese Prozesse visuell darstellen? Die Ergebnisse fügte die Künstlerin zu einem theatralisch inszenierten Parcours aus wissenschaftlichen, musealen, kindhaften und alltäglichen Zitaten zusammen und setzte sie für jeden Ort unterschiedlich um.

So gliederte sich die Ausstellung in Bremen räumlich in drei Teile: In einem klassisch weiß gestrichenen „Entrée" wurden großformatige Graphitzeichnungen präsentiert (*Hold Armor I (map)*, *Hold Armor II (map)*, *Pressure (map)*, *Common Carrier Case 1* und *Common Carrier Case 2 (Avatar)*). Im darauf folgenden Mittelteil entwickelten sich die Seitenwände des Raumes von vorne nach hinten von hellgrau zu tiefschwarz, um am Ende mittels eines schwarzen Bodenbelags die im Titel angedeutete Bühne und Keimzelle gleichermaßen zu schaffen. Hier dominierten der geschlossene *Giant Learning Cube* im Bühnenbereich, objekthafte *Speech Bubbles* an den Wänden, pfadartig ausgelegte schwarze Fußformen aus Holz auf dem Boden und die beiden Skulpturen *Common Carrier Case 1 (Präparat)* und *Common Carrier Case 2 (Präparat – Avatar)*, die Protagonisten gleich im Raum platziert waren. Die beiden letztgenannten Arbeiten nehmen die Oberfläche der gleichnamigen Zeichnungen auf Nesselstoff gedruckt auf und spannen sie zwischen zwei Glasscheiben ein. Gehalten wird die Anordnung von Händen mit Unterarmen aus Epoxidharz, zwischen denen das Glas eingespannt ist und deren Gestik zwischen offen-verletzlich bis geballt-aggressiv variiert. In ihrer Körperlichkeit erinnert die Oberfläche der kostümartig aufge-

Both versions of *Cube Cell Stage*, at the GAK as well as at the Kunstverein, are founded on questions as to the "HOW" of knowledge. "How to know?", sings Danz in one of her songs, which she also integrated into her *Rhyme and Reason* performance.[7] HOW does knowledge come to be? HOW is it communicated and assumed? HOW can one know what is factually correct and incorrect? And HOW can one visually represent these processes? The outcome of this inquiry was brought together by the artist into a theatrically staged sequence of scientific, museal, childlike, and everyday quotations, which were presented differently within each exhibition.

In Bremen the exhibition was divided into three different areas, each with its own architectural atmosphere. Large-format graphite drawings (*Hold Armor I (map)*, *Hold Armor II (map)*, *Pressure (map)*, *Common Carrier Case 1* and *Common Carrier Case 2 (Avatar)*) were presented in a classic, white-painted "anteroom." In the middle section, the side walls of the room transitioned from a light grey at the front to a deep black at the back, where an area dedicated to both the stage and cell of the exhibition's title was articulated by a black floor covering. This space was dominated by the closed *Giant Learning Cube* occupying a stage-like area, the object-like *Speech Bubbles* on the walls, a path-like series of wooden feet forms laid out on the floor and the sculptures *Common Carrier Case 1 (Präparat)* and *Common Carrier Case 2 (Präparat – Avatar)*, which were placed in the center of the space like protagonists. These two works entail prints on nettle-images of the drawings by the same titles. The prints are pressed between two sheets of glass, which are held in place by an arrangement of hands truncated at the lower arm, which are cast in epoxy resin. The gestures of the hands vary between open, vulnerable positions and balled, aggressive fists. In their physicalness the costume-like, puffed out cloth shapes recall tanned hides, the spanned preparations found in historical museums or anatomical collections. In the drawings the numerous representations from the fields of anatomy and language—body parts, organs, empty speech banners, and punctuation marks—recall tattoos and make the body into the carrier of subjective stories.

In the smaller adjacent room, another white-painted space, was a pyramid made of video documentations of Danz' previous performances and *Learning Cubes*, smaller versions of the *Giant Learning Cube*. They, too, borrow from the ABC blocks familiar from childhood and once again refer to the beginnings of all learning. The performance *Rhyme and Reason* also took up these conceptual threads. Taking place towards the end of the exhibition in Bremen, it activated a number of

bauschten Stoffe an abgezogene und präparatähnlich aufgespannte Häute wie im Historischen Museum oder in einer anatomischen Studie. Ihre zahlreichen Darstellungen aus den Bereichen Anatomie und Schrift – Körperteile, Organe, leere Spruchbänder oder Satzzeichen – lassen an Tätowierungen denken und machen den Körper zum Träger subjektiver Geschichten.

Im anschließenden, wieder hell gestrichenen Nebenraum fanden sich eine Pyramide aus Videodokumentationen von Danz' früheren Performances und *Learning Cubes*, kleinere Versionen des *Giant Learning Cube*. Auch sie zitieren die ABC-Würfel der Kindheit und verweisen einmal mehr auf die Anfänge allen Lernens. Diesen inhaltlichen Faden nahm auch die Performance *Rhyme and Reason* auf, die gegen Ende der Ausstellungslaufzeit in Bremen stattfand und einige Elemente des mittleren Raumes belebte: So wurde etwa die schwarze Wand wie eine raumfüllende Schultafel mit Kreide beschrieben und der *Giant Learning Cube* als monumentaler ABC-Würfel zum wichtigsten Requisit, indem er zunächst mehrfach erklärend um die eigene Achse gedreht und schließlich aufgeklappt wurde, um den Akteur/innen Platz auf dem dadurch entstehenden, potenzierten Bühnenraum zu bieten.

Die Ausstellung im Kunstverein Göttingen gestaltete sich in vielerlei Hinsicht als Antipode zur Präsentation der GAK, indem sie einen Großteil derselben Werke neu zusammenstellte und weiterentwickelte. War der ausschlaggebende Mittelteil in Bremen noch in dämmerndes Schwarz getaucht, bestand die Göttinger Version von *Cube Cell Stage* aus geradezu schmerzhaft grellem Weiß und Licht: „Es war eine erste Phase abgeschlossen und dadurch wurde es im Licht dargestellt. Das Suchen als Position zu zeigen, gibt auch eine Klarheit über das, was bis dahin erreicht war bzw. versagt blieb."[8] Ein weiterer wesentlicher Unterschied war die zentrale Installation um den *Giant Learning Cube*. Dieser fand sich in Göttingen in halb aufgeklapptem Zustand wieder und formte eine Art Präsentationshöhle für die Videodokumentation von *Rhyme and Reason* sowie einige Requisiten aus der Live-Performance: Drei Kostüme, Texte auf Folien und ein überdimensionierter Schlüssel aus Holz waren ebenso auf seinem Deckel abgelegt wie drei der *Learning Cubes* und der mit Buchstaben angefüllte Darmabguss von *Learning Organ (intestine)*. Die schwarzen Fußformen, in Bremen noch wie Pfade ausgelegt, kulminierten hier rund um den *Giant Learning Cube*, als seien etliche Personen suchend, in unterschiedlicher Richtung oder in einem endlosen Kreis um ihn herumgelaufen. Darüber hinaus integrierte *Cube Cell Stage* in Göttingen mit *Body/ydob, a flayed mirage* eine neue Arbeit, die sich aus der Bremer Performance

the elements in the middle area of the exhibition. For example, serving as a large scale classroom chalkboard, the black wall was written on with chalk, and the *Giant Learning Cube*, as a monumental ABC block, became the most important prop while being rotated around its own axis in the context of multiple explanations and then opened up and unfolded to offer the actors space on the potential stage that resulted.

In many aspects the exhibition at the Kunstverein Göttingen was the exact antipode of the presentation at the GAK, bringing together many of the same works in a new configuration and developing them further. Whereas the core middle space in Bremen was immersed in a dusky black, the Göttingen version of *Cube Cell Stage* was defined by an almost painfully bright white and light. "An initial phase had been completed and it was then placed in the light. Presenting the search itself as a position offered clarity about what had been achieved up until that point or what had remained a failure."[8] Another essential difference was the central installation surrounding the *Giant Learning Cube*, which in Göttingen was presented in a half opened position and formed a kind of presentation hollow for the video documentation of *Rhyme and Reason*. It also included a number of props from the live performance: three costumes, texts on plastic films, and an oversized key made of wood were arranged on its top along with three of the *Learning Cubes* and the cast of an intestine filled with letters, *Learning Organ (intestine)*. The black foot forms, which had been laid out like pathways in Bremen, were amassed here around the *Giant Learning Cube*, as if a number of people had been walking around it while searching in various directions or repeating an endless circle. In addition, *Cube Cell Stage* in Göttingen included a new work, *Body/ydob, a flayed mirage*, developed out of the performance in Bremen: a copper construction on which hung Danz' costume from the *Rhyme and Reason* performance. Dotted with children's drawings the piece of clothing hung like a cultic offering or a tattooed skin hung out to dry.

The representations on the cloth had been developed with an integrative school class during the Bremen exhibition. The children had been asked to create drawings of their ideas of the body and its organs. This project is exemplary of the numerous accompanying events in which the notions of the *Cube Cell Stage* were explored in depth. Outside a presentation or performance setting Danz tests additional formats for communicating and developing her ideas in process. Whereas in Bremen she held a workshop with children, in Göttingen she worked with educators in training. In addition to guided tours, as a classical form of mediating an exhibition, there was an artist talk, Prof. Hubert Knoblauch offered an

entwickelt hatte: ein kupferner Aufbau, an dem Danz' mit Kinderzeichnungen übersätes Kostüm aus *Rhyme and Reason* wie eine kultische Opfergabe oder zum Trocknen aufgehängte, tätowierte Haut hing.

Die Darstellungen auf dem Stoff wurden mit einer integrativen Schulklasse im Vorfeld der Bremer Ausstellung entwickelt, wobei die Kinder aufgefordert waren, ihre Vorstellungen vom Körper und seinen Organen zeichnerisch umzusetzen. Dieses Projekt steht beispielhaft für eine Vielzahl von Veranstaltungen, in denen *Cube Cell Stage* ausstellungsbegleitend vertieft wurde. Hier erprobte Mariechen Danz jenseits von Präsentation und Performance weitere Formate, um ihre Ideen zu kommunizieren und prozesshaft weiter zu entwickeln. Waren es in Bremen die Kinder, waren es in Göttingen Erzieher/innen in Ausbildung, mit denen die Künstlerin einen Workshop veranstaltete. Darüber hinaus fand neben Führungen als klassischer Form der Ausstellungsvermittlung ein Künstlergespräch statt, Prof. Hubert Knoblauch führte in die Essenz des Wissens aus Sicht der Soziologie ein und Sergej Parajanovs Film *The Color of Pomegranates* stellte eine visuelle Analogie zur Bildsprache der Ausstellung her. Eine wichtige Klammer bildete auch im Begleitprogramm von *Cube Cell Stage* die Musik, ebenfalls in Form verschiedener Strategien: Zur Eröffnung der Ausstellung in Bremen sang Danz eines ihrer Lieder a capella[10] und knüpfte so an die „oral tradition" an, die Tradition der mündlichen Weitergabe von Informationen als Kontrapunkt zu ihrer schriftlichen Niederlegung – mit dem gesungenen Text und seinem Refrain als Mittel der Erinnerungsstütze. In einem Konzert ihrer Band UNMAP wurden die Texte aus Danz' Performances dagegen in eine instrumentale Begleitung eingebettet und im Kontext der Popmusik verortet – nun mit dem Gedanken, Inhalte durch das akzeptierte Format und die Zugänglichkeit der Melodien zu kommunizieren.

Danz' Auseinandersetzung mit der phänomenologischen Seite des Wissens fußt auf zwei Aspekten, die sie auch in *Cube Cell Stage* gleichberechtigt nebeneinander stellte und immer wieder verzahnte: Sprache und Körper. Sprache ist ihr Möglichkeit, Wissen auszuformulieren und zu kommunizieren, die Brücke, über die man überhaupt miteinander in Beziehung tritt, aber auch potenzielle Quelle für Missverständnisse und Fehler: So zeigten sich in *Cube Cell Stage* lateinische Buchstaben auf den Seiten der verschieden großen *Cubes*, im feierlich aufgeschlagenen und doch unlesbaren *Book (unlearning) 1* und dem bunten Durcheinander von *Learning Organ (intestine)*. Die leeren Sprech- und Gedankenblasen, die an den Wänden der GAK zu sehen waren, lassen eine Vielzahl von Interpretationen zu: Warten sie darauf, von der Künstlerin oder den Besucher/innen gefüllt zu werden? Stehen sie für (inhalts)leere Kommunikation?

Learning Cubes TV Tower, 2012.
Installation view *Cube Cell Stage*, GAK
Gesellschaft für Aktuelle Kunst Bremen.

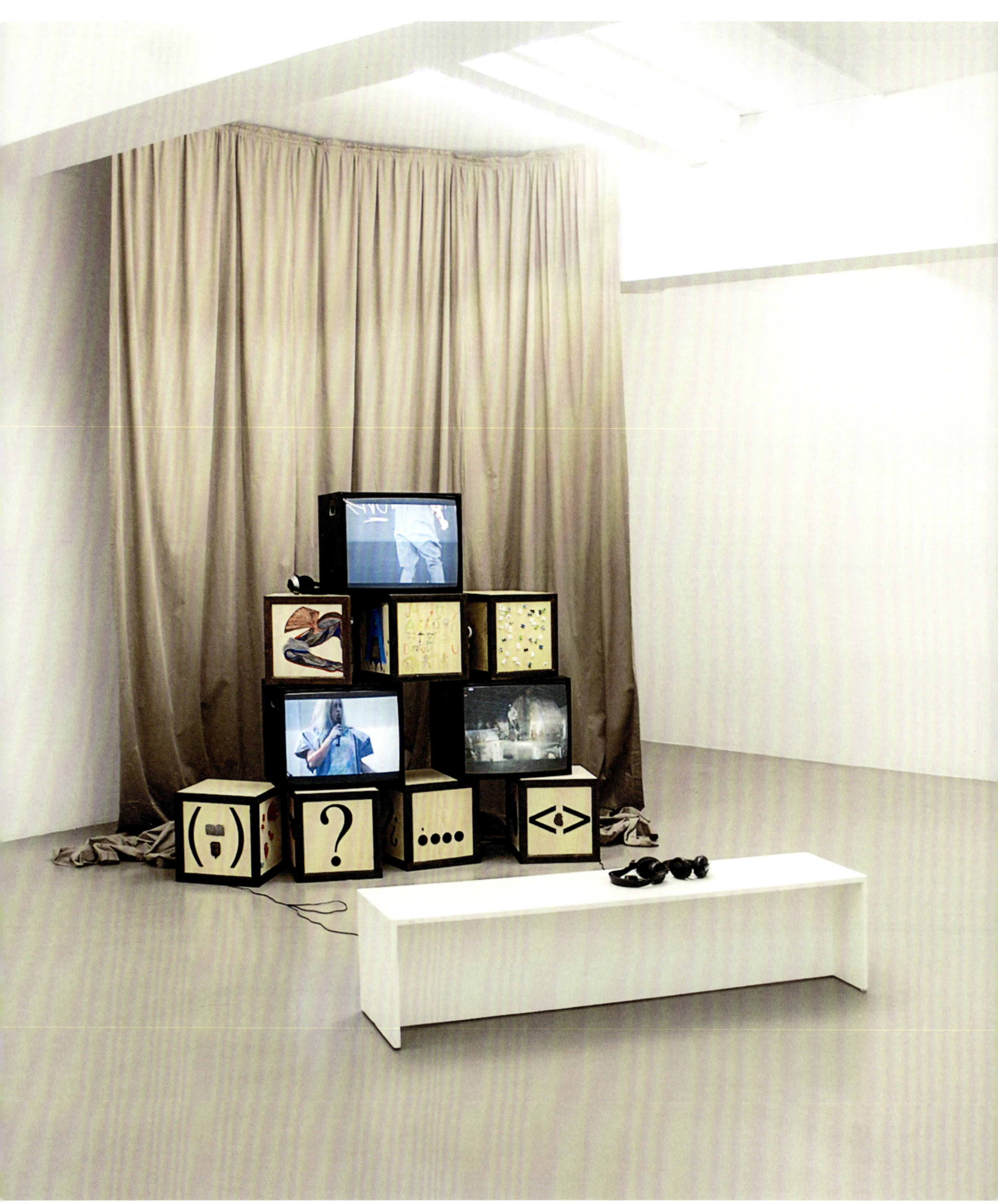

Sind ihre ursprünglichen Inhalte mittlerweile gelöscht?[11] Oder stellen sie Verbindungen zu anderen Epochen und Kulturen her – sind sie doch keineswegs ein Kind unserer zeitgenössischen Comics, sondern haben ihre Vorläufer beispielsweise in den Spruchbändern mittelalterlicher Darstellungen. An solche Gedanken anknüpfend integriert die Künstlerin diese in den verschiedenen Versionen der *Common Carrier Cases*.

Wie die *Learning Cubes* oder die als Schultafel fungierende schwarze Wand in *Cube Cell Stage* das Interesse für die Anfänge des Lernens markieren und Performance, Musikveranstaltungen, *Book (unlearning) 1* sowie Elemente der verschiedenen Zeichnungen den Gegensatz von gesprochener und schriftlicher Sprache fokussieren, knüpfen die Darstellungen der *Common Carrier Case*-Arbeiten an die visuellen Ausprägungen einer wortlosen Sprache an, die sich z. B. in Bildzeugnissen alter Kulturen zeigen. In Danz' Fokus stehen dabei vor allem die Völker des ehemaligen Mesoamerika (etwa die Maya oder Azteken). Wissen wurde hier in Bildern vermittelt, Sprache und visuelle Erscheinung waren eins. Die ebenfalls in *Cube Cell Stage* präsentierten Zeichnungen *Hold Armor I (map)*, *Hold Armor II (map)* und *Pressure (map)* erinnern dagegen an die uns vertraute Wissensvermittlung via Bildsprache auf großen Karten, wie sie bis heute in Schulen üblich ist. Allerdings zeigen die Karten bei Danz in sich verschlungene, nahezu unentschlüsselbare Körperbilder, statt die eine, einzig „wahre" anatomische Version in aller Klarheit vorzuführen.

Der Ort, an dem Sprache sich bildet – gesprochen, geschrieben oder verbildlicht –, ist der Körper. Der Körper ist der Beginn jeder Sprache. In anthropologischer Manier greift Danz in ihrer künstlerischen Produktion deshalb auf ihn zurück, vor allem und immer wieder in anatomisch anmutenden Darstellungen aus unterschiedlichen Epochen und Kontexten, aber auch in der übersteigerten Körperlichkeit ihrer Kostüme und *Common Carrier Case*-Skulpturen oder der In-Eins-Setzung von Körper und Sprache in Objekten wie *Learning Organ (intestine)*. Der Körper dient Danz als Ausgangspunkt für die Aneignung, Weitergabe und potenzielle Fehlerhaftigkeit von Wissen. Umgekehrt ist er seit Jahrhunderten selbst Untersuchungsgegenstand der Wissenschaft. In dieser Doppelrolle als Produzent und Reflexionsobjekt fungiert er in ihrer Arbeit. *Cube Cell Stage* war dementsprechend übersät mit anatomischen Darstellungen von menschlichen Organen und Gliedmaßen in allen Größen und

introduction to the *Essence of Knowledge* from a sociological perspective, and Sergej Parajanov's film *The Color of Pomegranates*[9] served as a visual analogy to the pictorial language of the exhibition. Music also served as an important thematic framework of the accompanying program of *Cube Cell Stage* with formats drawing on a range of strategies. At the opening of the exhibition in Bremen Danz sang one of her songs a capella,[10] thus creating a tie to oral traditions as a means of passing on information that "competed" with its written transmission—sung text and a refrain serve as mnemonic aids. In contrast, during a concert with her band UNMAP, Danz' texts from her performances were embedded in a pop music context—a reflection of her idea to communicate content through this accepted format and the immediacy of melodies.

Danz' concern with the phenomenological side of knowledge has two fundamental aspects that she placed on equal footing and side by side within *Cube Cell Stage* while also interlocking them—language and the body. To Danz language is the possibility of formulating and communicating knowledge, the bridge that allows us to establish relationships to one another; but it also poses a potential source for misunderstanding and mistakes. In *Cube Cell Stage* this is conveyed by the letters of the Latin alphabet found on the sides of the different sized cubes, in the book that solemnly lies open but is illegible, *Book (unlearning) 1*, and the bright-colored confusion of *Learning Organ (intestine)*. The empty speech and thought bubbles visible on the walls of the GAK permit a range of interpretations. Are they waiting to be filled in by the artist or the visitors? Do they represent communication that is emptied of content? Has the original context been removed?[11] Or do they create links to other eras or cultures? Such speech bubbles are by no means the offspring of contemporary comics but have their forerunners in the banners of text included in medieval imagery, for example. Drawing on such ideas, the artist integrates these forms in the various versions of the *Common Carrier Cases*.

Like the *Learning Cubes* or the black wall serving as a blackboard in *Cube Cell Stage*, which point to an interest in the earliest phases of learning, or like performance, music events, *Book (unlearning) 1* and elements of Danz' various drawings, which focus on the opposition of oral and written language, so the images of the *Common Carrier Case* works suggest the visual expression of a wordless language, as manifested in the visual

Common Carrier Case 2 (Präparat – Avatar), 2012. Installation view *Cube Cell Stage*, GAK Gesellschaft für Aktuelle Kunst Bremen.

Pages 21–23: *Footprints*, 2011; *3D Speech Bubble (blackboard) (small)*, 2012. Installation view *Cube Cell Stage*, GAK Gesellschaft für Aktuelle Kunst Bremen.

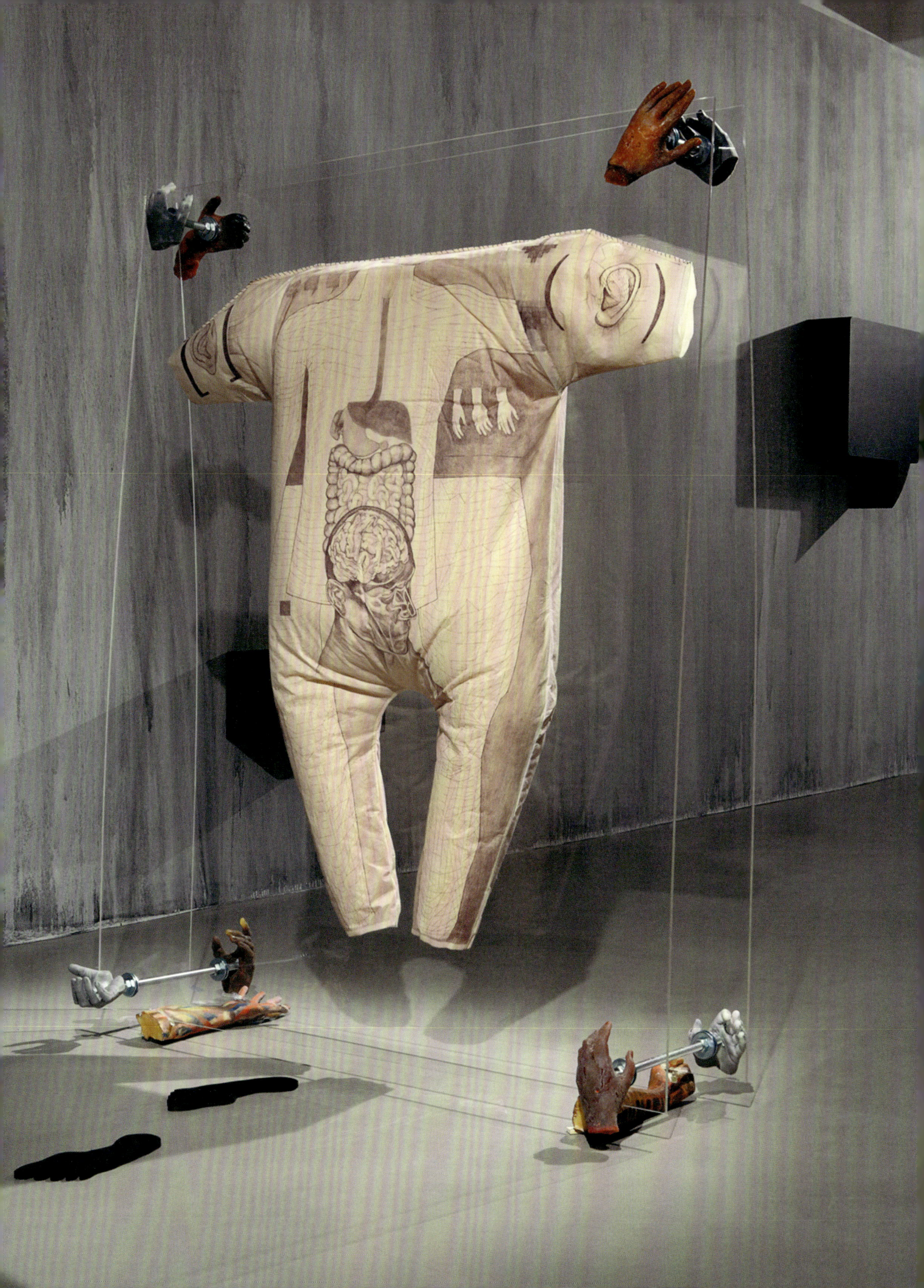

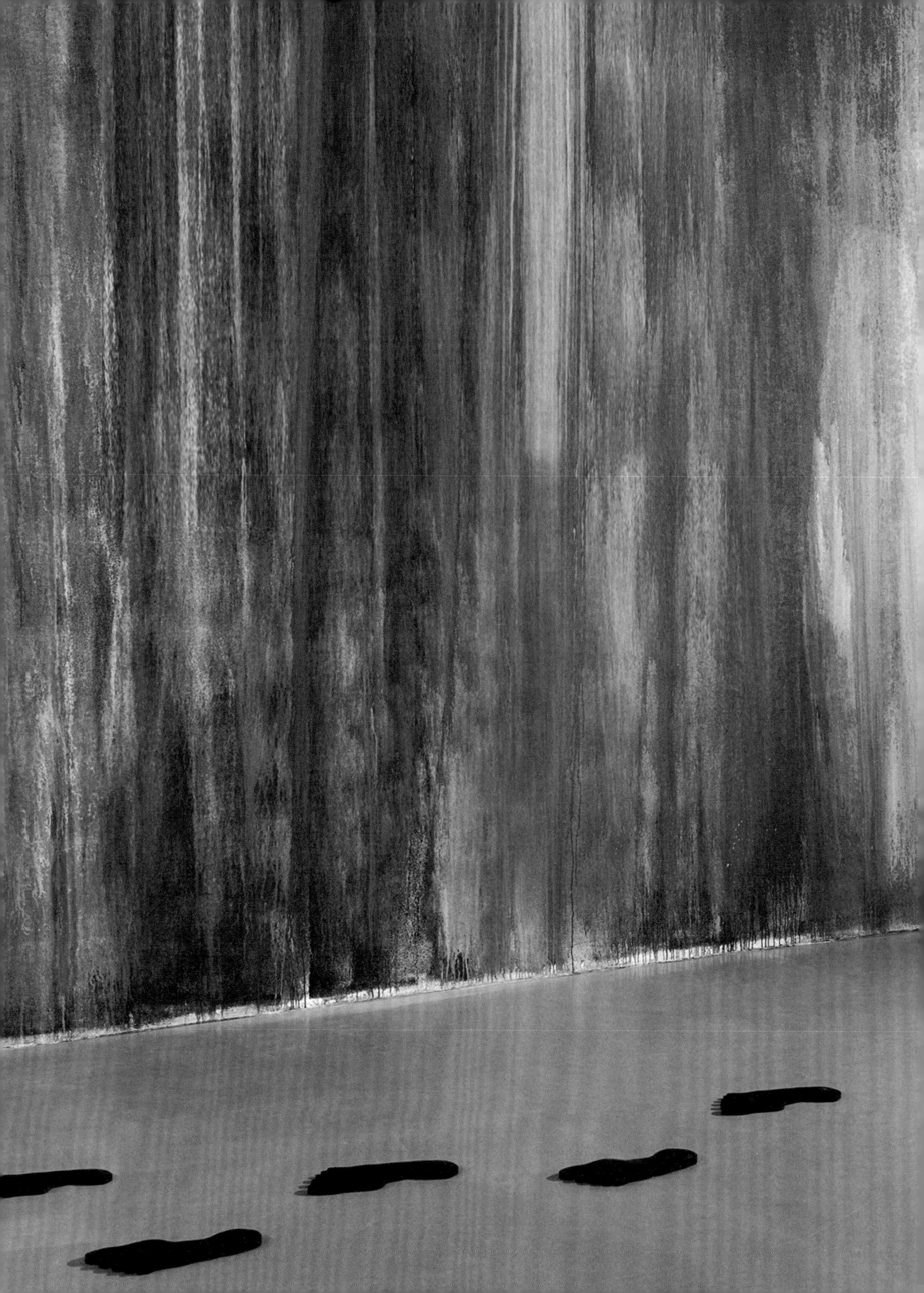

Materialitäten. Sie fanden sich in unterschiedlichen Abstraktionsgraden in den Graphitzeichnungen, lagen auf Sockeln oder klebten auf dem Boden und den *Cubes*. Abbilder von Gehirnen symbolisieren im Kosmos von Danz z.B. die Vermutung, die Annahme von etwas. Gleichzeitig stehen sie für Hierarchie selbst zwischen den menschlichen Organen, in deren Ranking das Gehirn als akzeptierter Sitz des Verstandes und der Reflexion in unserer Epoche den höchsten Stellenwert einnimmt. René Descartes etwa trennte im 17. Jahrhundert Körper und Verstand/Bewusstsein, löste damit das Gehirn als Reflexionswerkzeug aus dem Rest der menschlichen Organe heraus und etablierte das Mind-body-Problem. Auch die Neurologie verankert bis heute die Funktion des Bewusstseins allein im Gehirn. Nicht aber in der Welt von Mariechen Danz. Hier denkt und fühlt und reflektiert jedes Organ auf seine ihm eigene Weise: Der Darm etwa kann als Trichter/Verteiler und damit ebenfalls als Ort des Verständnisses gelesen werden. Ist er angefüllt mit Buchstaben wie in *Learning Organ (intestine)*, ist er „verstopft mit Sprache“[12]. Die Lunge dagegen kann Sitz potentieller Gifte sein. Hände wiederum nehmen in Danz' Arbeiten Verbindung zum Gegenüber auf, üben wortlose Kommunikation aus und halten (Skulpturen) fest (*Common Carrier Case 1 (Präparat)* und *Common Carrier Case 2 (Präparat – Avatar)*). Und die *Footprints* hinterlassen Spuren oder zeichnen Bewegungen vor, denen man folgen oder die man bewusst verlassen kann, um eigene Wege zu gehen – körperlich wie geistig.

Ein wiederkehrendes Missverständnis in der Rezeption von Danz' künstlerischem Denken ist die Einschätzung ihrer Person als „Performancekünstlerin“. Sicher ist, dass der Performance ein besonderer Stellenwert in ihrer Arbeit zukommt, bietet sie doch die einzigartige Möglichkeit, möglichst vielfältige Ausdrucksweisen miteinander zu verknüpfen: Text und Gesang, Objekt und Aktion, Kostüm, Malerei und Zeichnung. Sicher ist aber auch, dass die Entstehung einer Performance bei Mariechen Danz ein langwieriger, fast schmerzhafter Prozess ist, der sich nie losgelöst von dem Ausstellungszusammenhang lesen lässt, in dem er sich verortet. So auch bei *Rhyme and Reason*, ihrer zutiefst mit der Idee von *Cube Cell Stage* verbundenen Performance. In der Vorbereitung entwickelten sich zunächst die Graphitzeichnungen gleichermaßen als Ideenskizzen wie als eigenständige Werke. Darauf folgten die Entstehung der Skulpturen und Objekte und ihre kulissenhafte Anordnung im Raum. Die Performance selbst bildete den Kulminationspunkt in der künstlerischen Konzeption von *Cube Cell Stage* und hatte die Aufgabe, die anderen Medien zusätzlich zu aktivieren und ihre Inhalte auf einer erweiterten Ebene an die Besucher/innen zu transportieren – in Bremen als Live-Performance, in Göttingen als Videodokumentation

production of ancient cultures, for example. Danz focuses on the peoples of Mesoamerica (such as the Maya or the Aztecs). Also presented in *Cube Cell Stage*, the drawings *Hold Armor I (map)*, *Hold Armor II (map)* and *Pressure (map)* recall, in contrast, a familiar form of knowledge transfer through the visual language of large maps that are still common in schools today. However, Danz' maps convey contorted, almost indecipherable images of the body instead of presenting the one "true" anatomical version of the body in perfect clarity.

The site where language is formed—spoken, written, or visualized—is the body. The body is the beginning of every language. This is why Danz repeatedly turns to the body in an anthropological manner, largely through her repeated use of anatomically intoned imagery from various epochs and contexts as well as through the exaggerated physicality of her costumes and *Common Carrier Case* sculptures or in her equation of body and language in objects such as *Learning Organ (intestine)*. For Danz the body is a starting point for the appropriation, transmission, and potential faultiness of knowledge. At the same time, the body has served as an object of scientific investigation for centuries. In Danz' work the body assumes this dual role as both a producer and object of reflection. *Cube Cell Stage* was correspondingly filled with anatomical representations of human organs and limbs, portrayed in all sizes and materials. They were represented in various levels of abstraction in the graphite drawings; they lay on pedestals or were stuck to the floor and the *Cubes*. In Danz' cosmos, images of brains, for example, symbolize speculation, an assumption. They simultaneously also stand for the hierarchy among the human organs, a ranking in which the brain is considered the accepted seat of reason and reflection and thus is given the most significance in our era. In the 17th century René Descartes drew a separation between the body and the intellect, thus isolating the brain as a tool of reflection from the rest of the human organs and establishing the mind-body problem. And even today neurology still anchors the function of consciousness solely in the brain. But this does not apply in the world of Mariechen Danz. Here every organ thinks and feels and reflects in its own way. The intestine can be interpreted as a funnel or dispenser and thus also as a site of understanding. When filled with letters as in *Learning Organ (intestine)*, it is "constipated with language."[12] In contrast, the lung can be a place of potential poisons, whereas hands suggest a relationship to another person. They perform wordless communication and grasp things (i.e. sculptures, see *Common Carrier Case 1 (Präparat)* and *Common Carrier Case 2 (Präparat – Avatar)*). Also the *Footprints* leave tracks or indicate movements that one can follow or consciously deviate from, in order to go one's own path—both physically and conceptually.

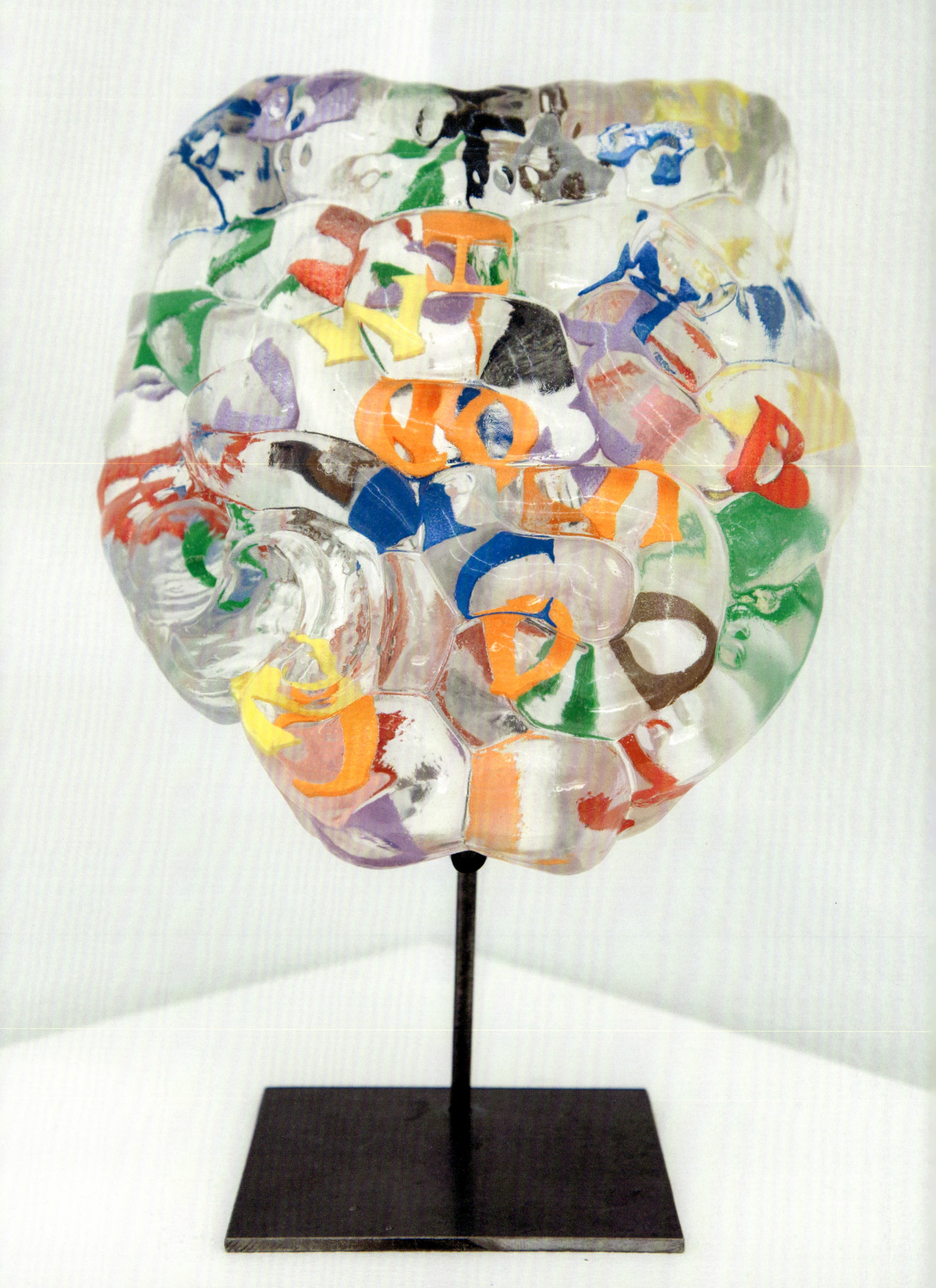

A repeated misunderstanding in the reception of Danz' artistic concept is the idea that she is a "performance artist." Certainly performance does play a particular role in her work, since it is a unique means of bringing together highly diverse forms of expression—text and song, object and action, costume, painting, and drawing. The development of a performance is a protracted and almost painful process for her, which is not be considered independent of the exhibition context, from which it originated. This is also the case with *Rhyme and Reason*, the performance intrinsically linked with the *Cube Cell Stage* project. In preparing the exhibition Danz first developed the graphite drawings, both as conceptual sketches and independent works. The sculptures and objects and their scene-like placement in the exhibition space emerged next. The performance itself served as the culmination point of the artistic conception underlying *Cube Cell Stage* and served to further activate other media and transport the context of the work to visitors on another level—in Bremen as a live performance, in Göttingen as a video documentation surrounded by the props used in the performance. In opposition to drawings, objects, or installations, a performance does not stand alone in Danz' work but requires the aggregate combination of various genres. In *Rhyme and Reason* ornately costumed actors encountered one another in an already existent installation. The actors followed a plot and were accompanied by chant. Herself a protagonist, Danz provided impulses for a play between prescribed action and improvisation. In doing so, she once again challenged the hierarchies of knowledge systems by assuming different speaker roles and constantly changing back and forth from acting as a teacher and as a student. *Rhyme and Reason* resembles a contemporary mini opera, raising questions about systems of order, modes of communication, the formation of language, symbols of power, and, repeatedly, the notion of "how to know." The performance incorporated the images, body parts, and speech bubbles that were already on site and added new elements to them.

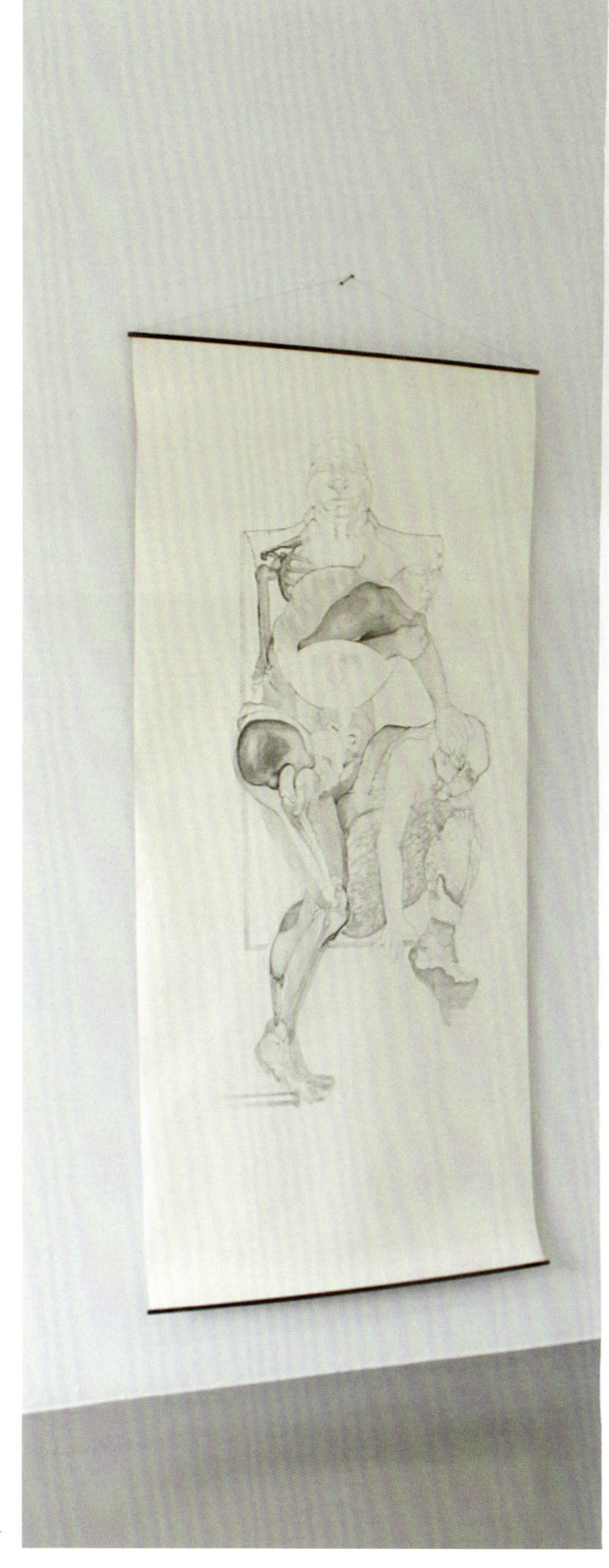

Page 25: *Learning Organ (intestine)*, 2012.

f.l.t.r.: *Pressure (map)*, 2010; *Hold Armor I (map)*, 2007–2010; *Hold Armor II (map)*, 2007–2010. Installation view *Cube Cell Stage*, GAK Gesellschaft für Aktuelle Kunst Bremen.

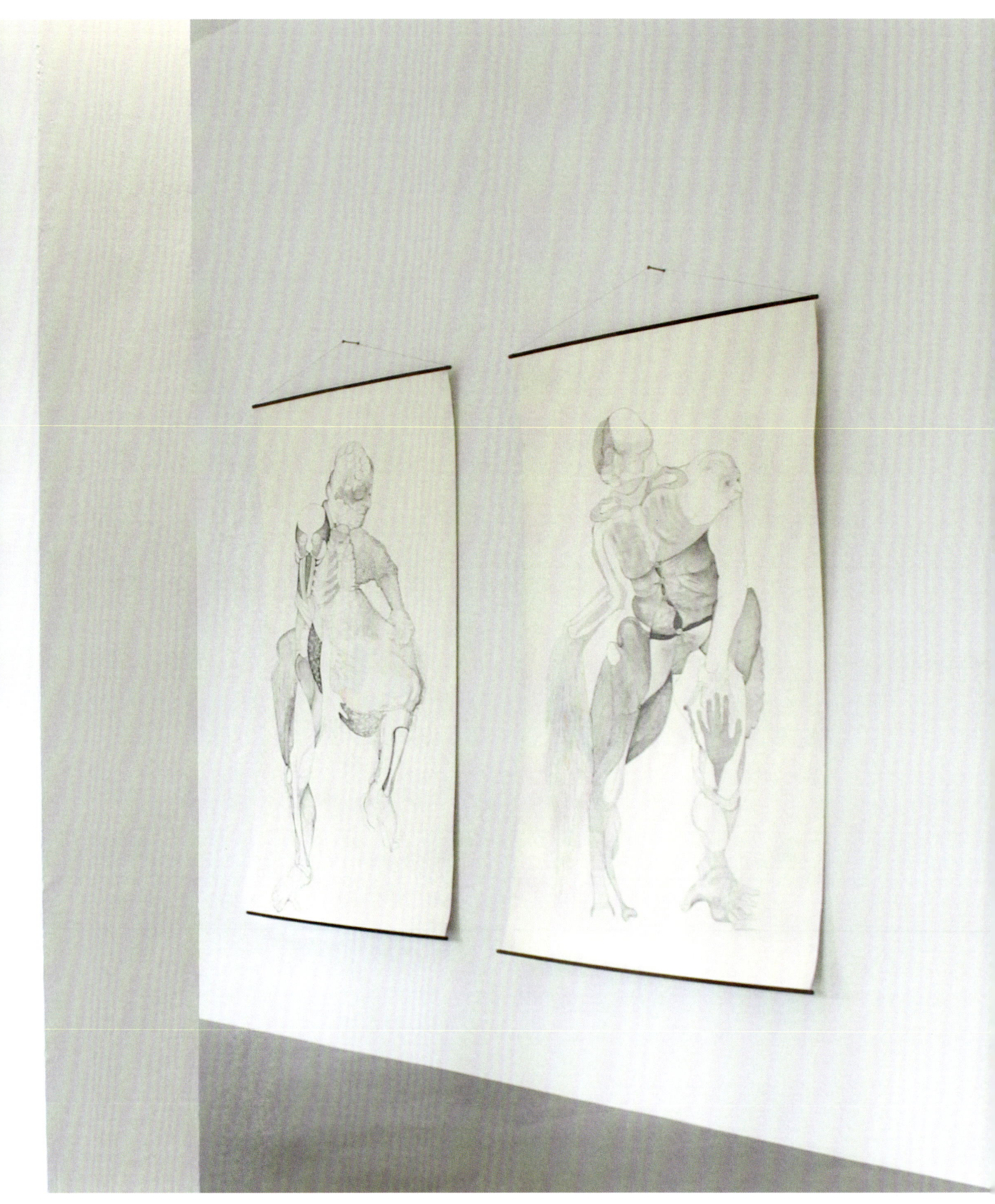

umgeben von den in ihr genutzten Requisiten. Doch kann die Performance, ganz im Gegensatz zu Zeichnung, Objekt oder Installation, in der Arbeit von Danz nicht für sich allein stehen, sondern benötigt den Zusammenschluss der verschiedenen Gattungen. In *Rhyme and Reason* trafen innerhalb des bereits existierenden installativen Rahmens üppig kostümierte Darsteller/innen aufeinander, die einem Plot folgten und von Gesang begleitet wurden. Danz selbst gab als Protagonistin die Impulse für das Spiel zwischen festgelegter Handlung und Improvisation. Dabei hinterfragte sie einmal mehr die Hierarchien von Wissenssystemen, indem sie verschiedene Sprecherpositionen einnahm und beständig zwischen Lehrer- und Schülerrolle hin- und her wechselte. *Rhyme and Reason* erinnerte an eine zeitgenössische Mini-Oper und formulierte Fragestellungen nach Ordnungssystemen, Kommunikationsweisen, Sprachbildung, Machtinsignien und immer wieder dem „How to know?". Als Requisiten bediente sich die Performance der Bilder, Körperteile und Sprechblasen, die bereits im Setting vorhanden waren, und fügte ihnen neue Elemente hinzu.

Ob nun Performance, Installation, Gesang, Zeichnung, Malerei, Objekt, Film oder ihr Zusammenspiel im Ausstellungszusammenhang: Das künstlerische Schaffen von Mariechen Danz ist mit seinen vielfältigen Äußerungsformen ein sich ständig fortschreibendes Abarbeiten an den Missverständnissen, Leerstellen, Platzhaltern, Geschichten und Neuerfindungen von Wissen. Es speist sich gleichwertig aus allen Quellen, derer die Künstlerin habhaft werden kann, und macht keinen Unterschied etwa zwischen anatomischen Darstellungen aus der Medizin, Kinderzeichnungen, aztekischen Gottheiten oder Popsongs. Der Körper ist der Ausgangspunkt aller Wissensproduktion, die Sprache ihr Vermittlungsorgan. Beide nutzt Mariechen Danz in der Erkenntnis, dass in dem Versuch, die hierarchische Struktur, die Subjektivität und potenzielle Fehlerhaftigkeit jeder Äußerung zu umgehen, nur Fragen möglich sind – und niemals endgültige Antworten.

1 Refrain von *Take Over*, UNMAP 2013, s. hier S. 70.
2 Wobei: „A territory can be a system of any kind, conceptional, linguistic, social, or affective.", s. Paul Patton, *Deleuzian Concepts: Philosophy, Colonization, Politics*, Stanford 2010, S. 52.
3 „The severance of social, political, or cultural practices from their native places and populations.", s. http://oxforddictionaries.com/definition/deterritorialization, 11. Oktober 2013.
4 S. http://www.medscape.com/viewarticle/769263_8, 28. Oktober 2013.
5 S. Brian O'Doherty, *Inside the White Cube*, 1976, und die daran anschließenden Debatten.
6 z.B. *Süden*, Deutsche Bank KunstHalle, Berlin 2013.
7 *How to know*, UNMAP 2011.
8 Mariechen Danz in einer E-Mail an die Autorin, 24. September 2013.
9 *The Color of Pomegranates*, R. Sergej Parajanov, 78 min. (armen. Version), 72. Min. (sowj. Überarbeitung), Farbe, Ton, UdSSR 1968.
10 *Chalk*, UNMAP 2011, s. hier S. 68.
11 „An ‚empty' speechbubble is not waiting – it signifies what has been erased, what has been omitted – and what the WORDED form can not contain. It Is a blackboard, it can be repeatedly rewritten...", Mariechen Danz in *Rhyme and Reason*, Performance am 24. Mai 2012 in der GAK Gesellschaft für Aktuelle Kunst Bremen.
12 Mariechen Danz im Gespräch mit der Autorin, März 2012.

Whether performance, installation, song, drawing, painting, objects, film, or the interplay of multiple genres in an exhibition context, the artistic oeuvre of Mariechen Danz is in its manifold manifestations an ongoing confrontation with the misunderstandings, omissions, stand-ins, stories, and inventions of knowledge. Her work draws indiscriminately from all possible sources available to the artist, who values medical anatomical illustrations, children's drawings, Aztec divinities, and the general appeal of pop songs equally. The body is the source of all knowledge production, and language is its means of transmission. Mariechen Danz uses both in the realization that the attempt to circumvent the hierarchical nature, subjectivity and potential falsity of every statement only gives rise to questions—never definite answers.

1 Refrain from *Take Over*, UNMAP 2013, see here p. 70.
2 But "a territory can be a system of any kind, conceptional, linguistic, social, or affective." See Paul Patton, *Deleuzian Concepts: Philosophy, Colonization, Politics*, Stanford 2010, p. 52.
3 See http://oxforddictionaries.com/definition/deterritorialization, October 11, 2013.
4 See http://www.medscape.com/viewarticle/769263_8, October 28, 2013.
5 See Brian O'Doherty, *Inside the White Cube*, 1976, and subsequent debates.
6 For example, the exhibition *Süden*, Deutsche Bank KunstHalle, Berlin 2013.
7 *How to know*, UNMAP 2011.
8 Mariechen Danz in an email to the author, September 24, 2013.
9 *The Color of Pomegranates*, R. Sergej Parajanov, 78 min. (Armenian version), 72 min. (Soviet revision), color, sound, UdSSR 1968.
10 *Chalk*, UNMAP 2011, see here p. 68.
11 "An 'empty' speech bubble is not waiting—it signifies what has been erased, what has been omitted—and what the WORDED form can not contain. It's a blackboard, it can be repeatedly rewritten...," extract from *Rhyme and Reason*, performance on May 24 2012 at GAK Gesellschaft für Aktuelle Kunst Bremen.
12 Mariechen Danz in a conversation with the author, March 2012.

Pressure (map) (detail), 2010.

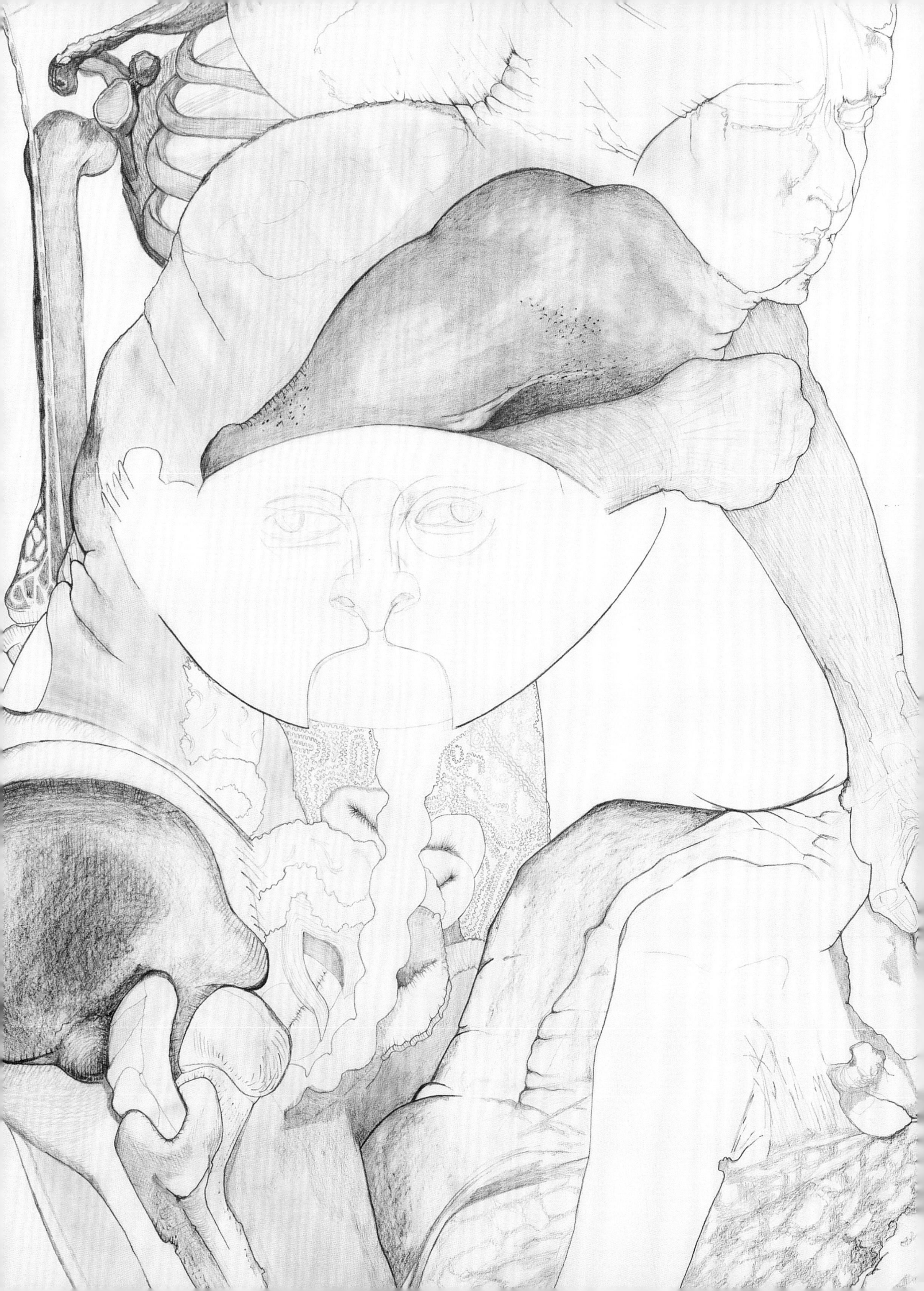

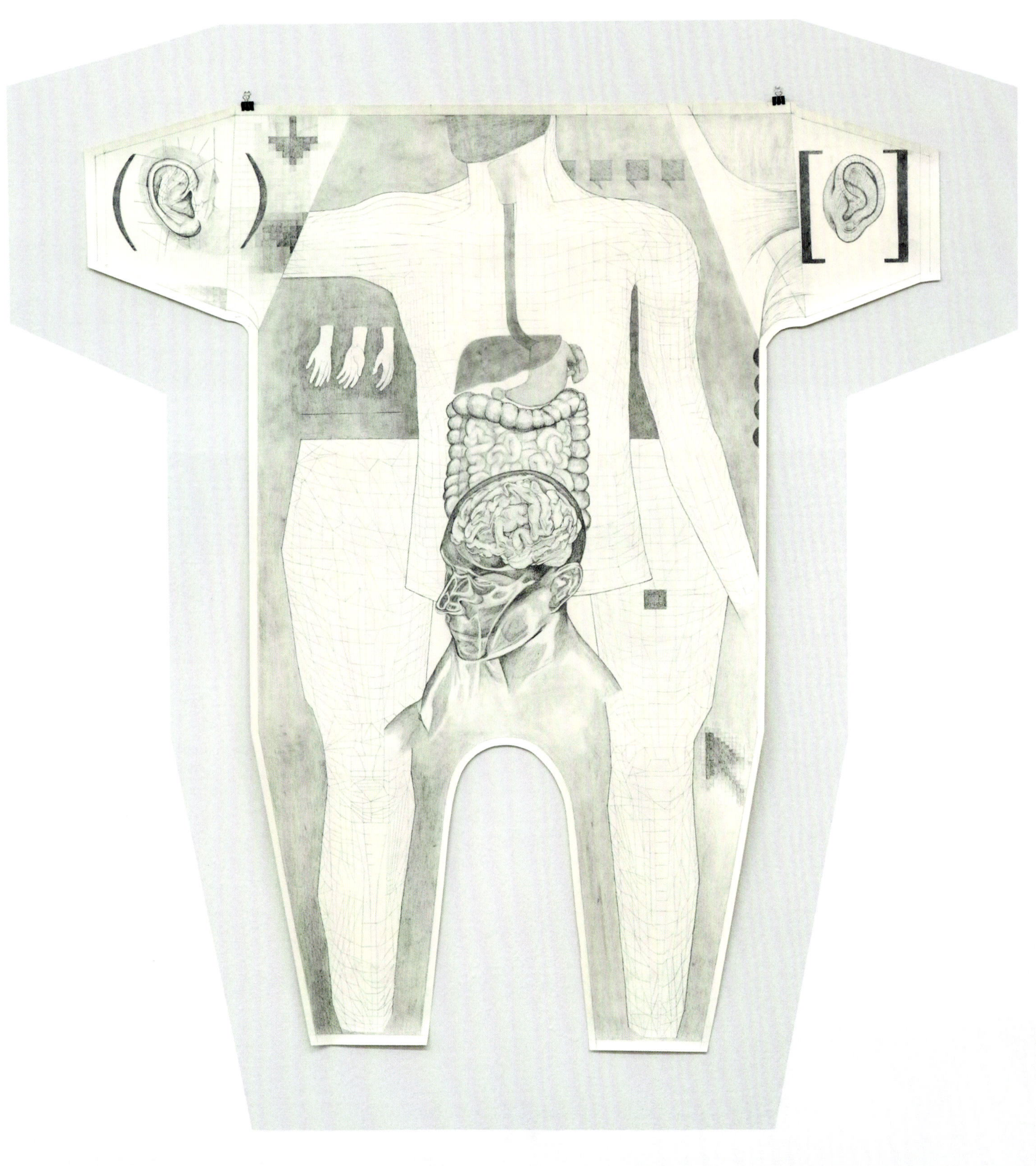

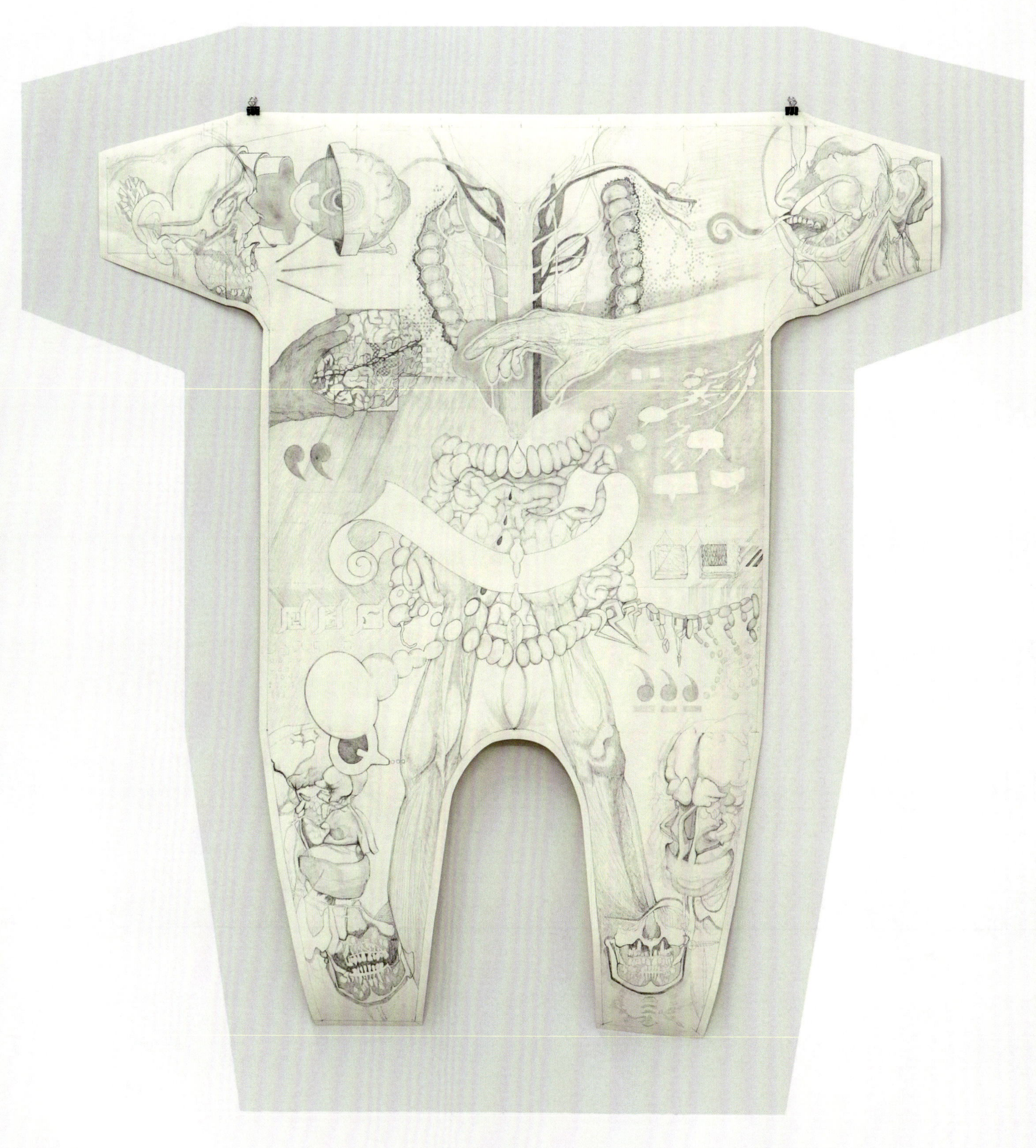

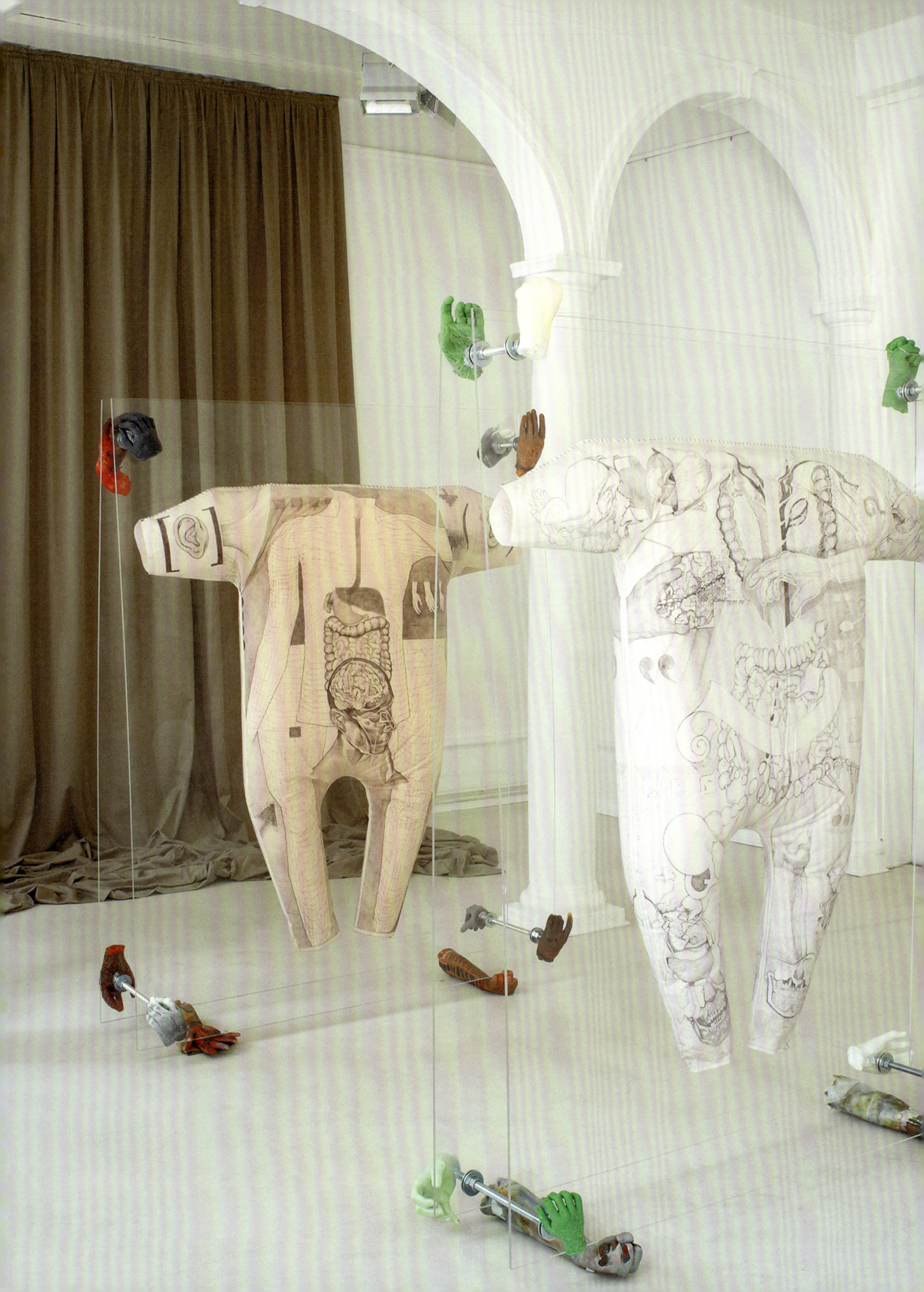

Common Carrier Case 2 (Präparat – Avatar), 2012 (back);
Common Carrier Case 1 (Präparat), 2011 (front).
Installation view *Cube Cell Stage*, Kunstverein Göttingen.

Pages 30–31:
f.l.t.r.: *Common Carrier Case 2 (Avatar)*, 2012; *Common Carrier Case 1*, 2011.
Installation view *Cube Cell Stage*, GAK Gesellschaft für Aktuelle Kunst Bremen.

Pages 34–35:
Common Carrier Case 1 (Präparat) (detail), 2011.

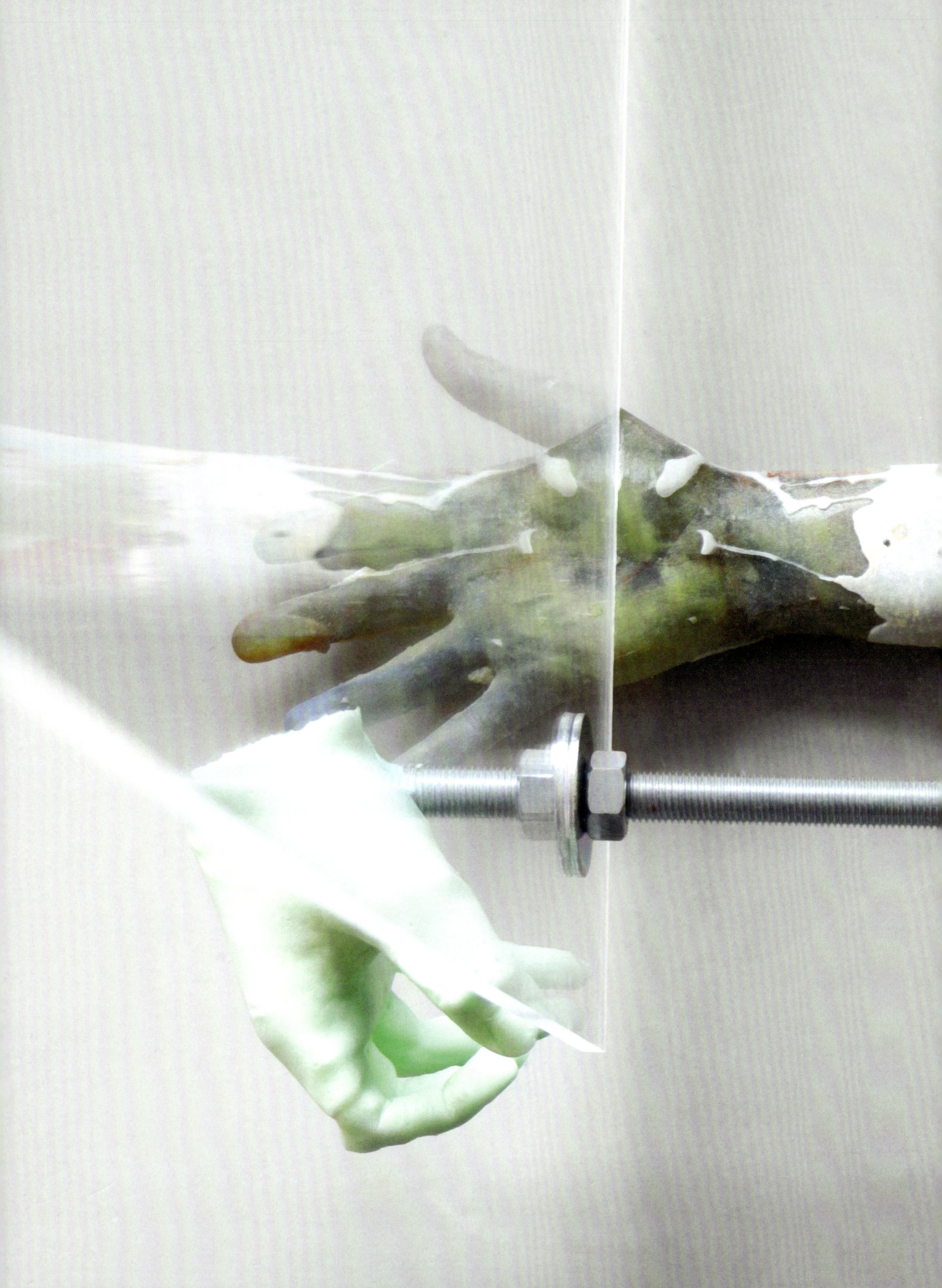

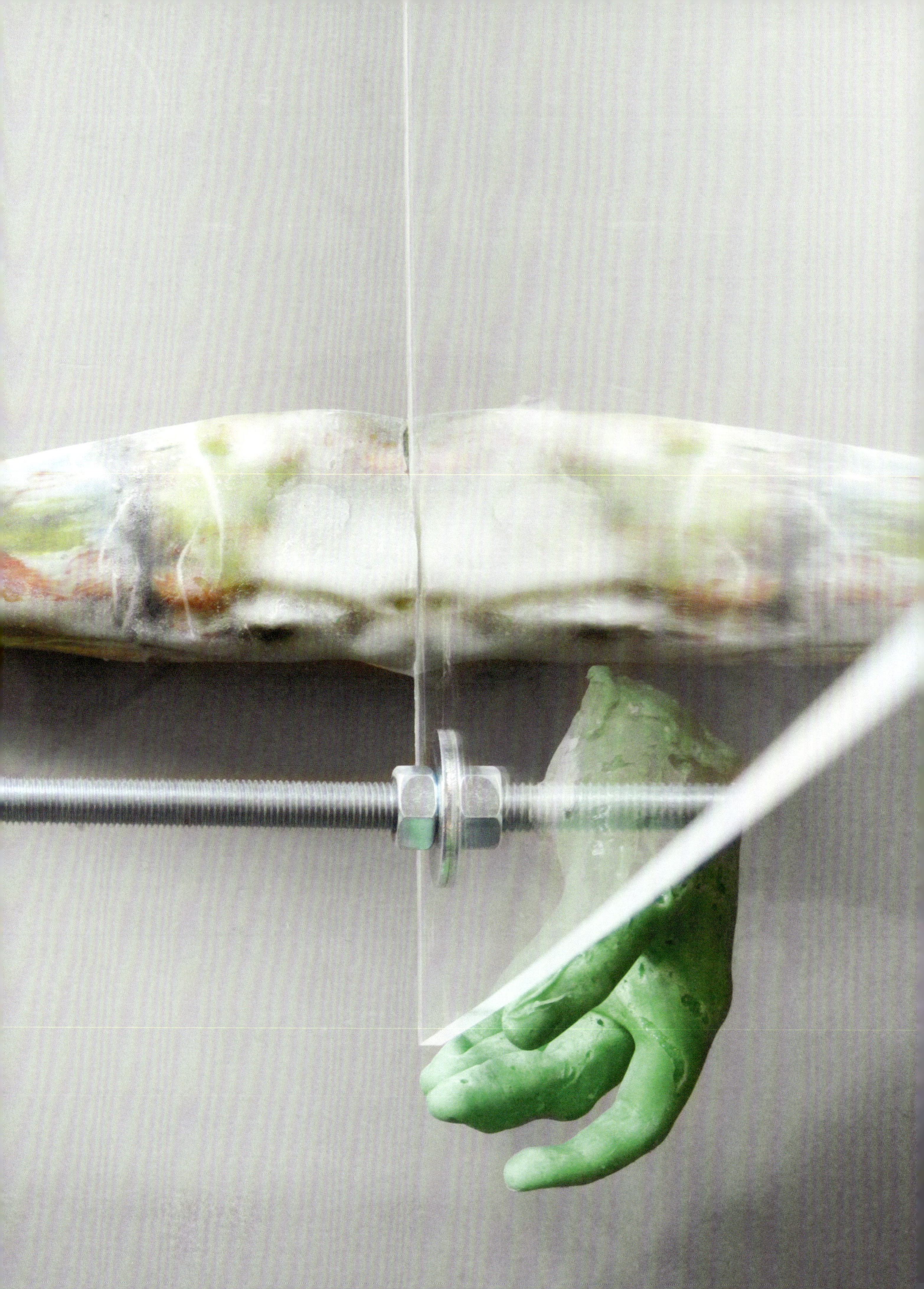

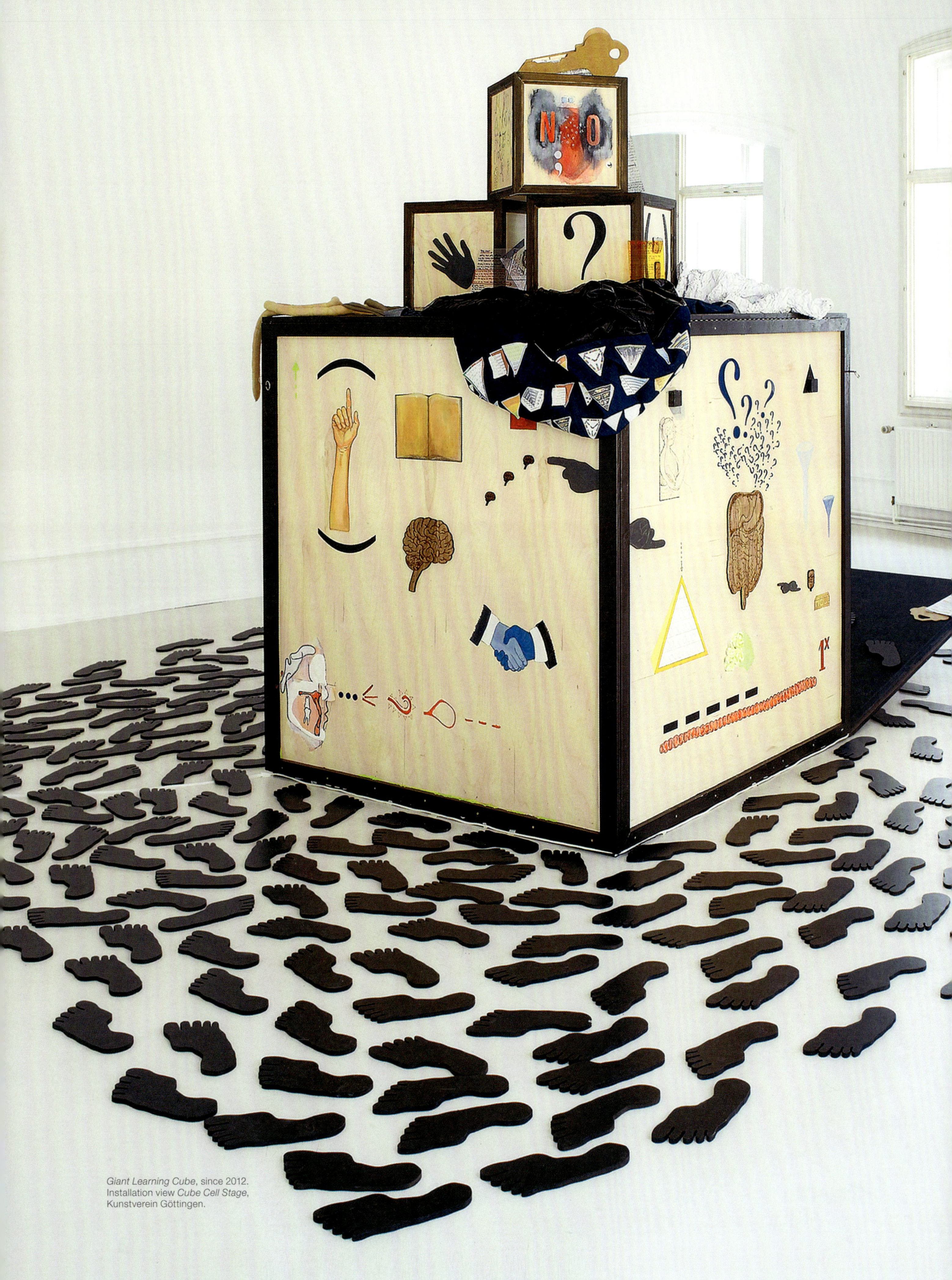

Giant Learning Cube, since 2012.
Installation view *Cube Cell Stage*,
Kunstverein Göttingen.

DIE GEOMETRIE VON KÖRPER UND GEIST
BODY MIND GEOMETRY

LAURA SCHLEUSSER

Giant Learning Cube, ein gleichförmiger, geometrischer Körper, Baustein oder Unterrichtsmittel, Wissensbehälter oder -träger, ist das Herzstück von Mariechen Danz' *Cube Cell Stage*. Das flexible Gebilde kann geöffnet und auseinandergeklappt werden. Es ist eine prozessorientierte Arbeit mit einer eindrucksvollen Präsenz, die an jedem neuen Ausstellungsort weiter entwickelt wird. Die aus der Früherziehung bekannten hölzernen ABC-Bauklötze standen für den Würfel Modell, doch seine Maße würden jedes Kind in den Schatten stellen. Die schwarzen Ränder, mit denen die Flächen der einfachen Sperrholzkonstruktion eingerahmt sind, verleihen dem Kubus zunächst eine imposante, wenn nicht bedrohliche Ausstrahlung. Statt klarer einzelner Buchstaben in Primärfarben sind seine Seiten mit Symbolen auf neutralem Grund übersät: Körperteile, anatomische Darstellungen, grammatikalische Zeichen, zeigende Gesten, Diagramme, Linien, Pfeile, Abdrücke und Markierungen.

Die unmittelbare Funktion des übergroßen und aus einfachen Materialien gebauten Würfels ist die der Requisite. Danz zufolge ist er bis dato das einzige Werk, das sie speziell für einen Perfomance-Zusammenhang geschaffen hat: Der Würfel steht im Mittelpunkt der Performance und des Videos *Rhyme and Reason*. Das Schwarz seiner Kanten, das von der Tafelfarbe in seinem Inneren aufgegriffen wird, lässt sich als Bühnenschwarz lesen. Dass sich der Würfel flach auseinanderfalten lässt und so eine neutrale Bühne im Hüpfkastenmuster ergibt, ist entscheidend dafür, wie die Performance, genauer, der Performance-Raum zu einem Umfeld wird, in dem Danz viele ihrer Ideen verhandelt, wo sie ihrer eindringlichen Kritik an den etablierten Wissenssystemen eine Stimme verleiht.

A uniform, geometric solid, a building block or instructional tool, a container and carrier of meaning, the *Giant Learning Cube* is the core structure of Mariechen Danz' *Cube Cell Stage*. A flexible structure that can be opened and unfolded. A work in progress that is continually being added to with each exhibition venue, the cube has a commanding presence. Although clearly modeled on the traditional wooden ABC building blocks that are standard early learning tools, its dimensions would dwarf any child. The black borders framing each side of the simple plywood structure initially give the cube an imposing and even intimidating aura. Instead of having clear, single letters in primary colors, its sides are covered with a profusion of symbols set against a neutral background—body parts, anatomical renderings, grammatical signs, pointing gestures, diagrams, lines, arrows, impressions, and markings.

Oversized and made of simple materials, the cube's immanent function is that of a prop. According to Danz, it is the only work she has yet specifically created for a performance context, and the cube is a focal object in the live performance and video *Rhyme and Reason*. The black of its edges, which is carried over into the chalkboard paint of the interior, can thus be read as a theatrical black. That the cube can be folded out flat to form a neutral stage in a hop-scotch pattern is key to how performance or, more specifically, the space of performance serves as a realm in which so many of Danz' ideas are negotiated and her pressing challenges to established systems of knowledge are voiced.

When standing isolated and closed, the cube does not reveal this performative potential. Instead, it appears almost monolithic.

Für sich geschlossen dastehend, enthüllt der Kubus sein performatives Potenzial nicht. Er erscheint fast als Monolith. Auf seiner Oberfläche begegnen wir einem Puzzle von frei platzierten Piktogrammen, die keiner ersichtlichen Ordnung oder klaren Komposition folgen. Mit den verschiedenen Satzzeichen und Handgesten wird zweifelsfrei eine Sprache angedeutet – doch welche Sprache, welchen Ursprungs? Auf einer der Würfelseiten ist ein Symbol für Händeschütteln dargestellt, eine dunkle und eine helle Hand, die sich aus Anzugärmeln entgegenstrecken – auf ein weltweites Abkommen. Landkartenteile ergießen sich in einem die Erdkugel andeutenden Bogen über eine andere Seite. Signalisieren, zeigen, hinweisen: Zeigefinger lenken unsere Blicke. Anatomische Zeichnungen zerlegen und zerschneiden den Körper, wie um einzelne Funktionen zu verdeutlichen und zu analysieren.

Doch *Giant Learning Cube* von Danz illustriert und erklärt nicht. Statt uns in einer Art visuellem Esperanto zu unterrichten, konfrontiert uns das Werk mit Verwirrung. Trotz der Klarheit der einzelnen Darstellungen und Zeichen bleiben die Symbole, die sich in mehreren, teils überlappenden Schichten mit der Zeit auf den Tafelflächen des Würfels angehäuft haben, undurchdringlich. Ein kohärentes Narrativ wird man hier nicht finden. Wie bei einigen anderen Werken von Danz erinnert das Format des geschlossenen Kubus an ein Spiel, scheint eine Herausforderung darzustellen. Geht man um den Würfel herum, um eine Öffnung oder einen Eingang zu finden, gewinnt man den Eindruck, man müsse einen Code knacken, ein Rätsel lösen, das Geheimnis in seinem Inneren lüften.

Bei genauerem Hinsehen bemerkt man allerdings bald, dass das visuelle Vokabular von Danz nicht der Logik eines Verschlüsselungssystems folgt. Tatsächlich zeigt sich oft eine Verneinung jedweder Art von Logik oder Hierarchie, selbst auf grammatikalischer Ebene. Wie die schrittweise entstehende Komposition auf dem Kubus selbst kommuniziert seine Bildsprache Offenheit, Prozesshaftigkeit und die Ablehnung einer etablierten Ordnung. In den Zeilen eines Klassenbuchs sind z. B. Buchstaben durch Körperteile ersetzt und von rechts nach links deutende Hände leiten das Auge zum „Rückwärtslesen" an. Eine Wolke aus Fragezeichen ist zu sehen, Miniaturgehirne in einer Reihe mögen für die drei Punkte eines unfertigen Gedankens stehen, eine Folge von Unterstrichen für einen Lückentext. Illustrationen, vereinfachte Zeichnungen, Symbolbilder – die Grafiken, die den Würfel bedecken, sind augenscheinlich didaktisch, eine eindeutige Aussage ist jedoch in keiner Form zu finden. Die selbstbewusste, lautstarke Geste einer aufwärts zeigenden Hand steht in Klammern, wird unter Vorbehalt gestellt. Ein pyramidenförmiges Diagramm mit

On its surface we are presented with a puzzle of free-floating pictograms arranged in no discernable order or clear-cut compositional structure. With various punctuation marks and gesturing hands, the imagery clearly suggests a language, but which language, of what origin? On one side a pair of shaking hands—one dark and one light, both extending from business suits—suggests a system of global agreement. Elsewhere we find pieces of a map cascading down one side in an arch that suggests the sphere of the earth. Indicating and showing, pointing fingers direct the gaze. Anatomical drawings dissect and slice through the body, as if to clarify and analyze isolated functions.

But instead of illustrating and explaining, instead of instructing us in a version of visual Esperanto, Danz' cube confronts us with confusion. Despite the clarity of individual representations and signs, the symbols amassed on the cube's outer panels—added to and layered upon one another over time—remain impenetrable; they offer no coherent narrative. Like a number or Danz' works, the format of the closed cube seems to recall a game, and it appears to present a challenge. Circling the cube to find an opening or entry, one has the sense of needing to crack the code, solve the riddle, and unlock the mystery within.

Examining the sum of images more closely, one soon realizes, however, that Danz' visual vocabulary does not follow the logic of an encrypted system. In fact, it often indicates a negation of any kind of logic or hierarchy, even grammatical. Just like the gradually emerging composition on the cube, its scattered imagery conveys open-endedness, process, and a rejection of established order. For example, on the lines of a school ledger, parts of the body replace letters, and hands pointing from right to left direct the eye to perform a "backwards" reading. One finds a cloud of questions marks, a series of miniature brains forming the dot-dot-dot of an unfinished idea, and a row of fill-in-the-blank dashes. Illustrations, simplified drawings, icons—the graphics covering the cube are obviously didactic, yet they avoid any form of definitive statement. The confident, exclamatory gesture of an upward pointing hand is bracketed and made conditional. A pyramid-shaped diagram is inscribed with arrows indicating the top-down/bottom-up struggles inherent in a hierarchical structure. Repetition, simultaneity, a purging of script and symbolic authorities are mediated by this conflation of signs. Despite all of Danz' visual cues, we are confronted with a semiotic breakdown that leaves us with an impression of scatteredness, irregularity, and a lack of correspondence. Are we supposed to piece this all together?

Pfeilen deutet auf die widerstreitenden Kräfte hin, die Teil jeder hierarchischen Struktur sind. Wiederholung, Gleichzeitigkeit, eine Reinigung der Schrift und symbolischer Autoritäten werden in dieser Verschmelzung von Zeichen verhandelt. Trotz der vielen visuellen Hinweise, die uns Danz gibt, stehen wir einem semiotischen Breakdown gegenüber, der in uns den Eindruck von Zerfaserung, Ungereimtheit und Bezugslosigkeit hinterlässt. Sollen wir das etwa alles zusammensetzen?

Für Danz ist diese „Unleserlichkeit" des Kubus Absicht und zentrales Thema. Versagen, Zusammenbruch und der Frust der Fehlkommunikation sind Kernprobleme in *Cube Cell Stage*, wie in Danz' Werk überhaupt. Indem sie die Aufdringlichkeit von Sprache oder Informationsstrukturen als koloniale Praktiken anspricht, bei denen Bezeichnen und Definieren zu Akten eines Autoritätsanspruchs werden, versucht Danz diese Prozesse immer wieder zu durchbrechen. Deshalb greift sie so häufig auf Methoden zurück, die nicht Teil des traditionellen Kanons sind: auf mündliche Überlieferungen, Lieder, Bildsprache und vor allem auf eine Nivellierung und Verwirrung bestehender Ordnungen. Wie man am Aussehen des Würfels erkennen kann, werden dabei Klarheit und Eindeutigkeit, lineare Erzählstruktur und Kohärenz geopfert. Und dennoch, wie der Chor der gestikulierenden Finger mit offenbarer Dringlichkeit zeigt: Der Würfel soll etwas kommunizieren.

Eins steht fest: Der Körper ist für das, was Danz uns sagen will, von zentraler Bedeutung. Mittig auf vier Seiten des Würfels angebracht, wirken wichtige Organe des menschlichen Körpers wie Touch-Keys. Die zentralen Symbolbilder sind aus dunklem Walnussholz gemacht: Lungen, Herz, Verdauungssystem und Gehirn. Jedes einzelne wird aktiviert durch die dicht um sie gestreute Menge visueller Elemente. Auf einer der Tafeln beispielsweise scheinen Fragezeichen durch den Magen und Darm getrichtert und als hirnartige, gereinigte weiße Masse ausgeschieden zu werden. Verständnis ist anscheinend ein Verdauungsprozess. Das Herz steht in Anführungszeichen, während mehrere Linien darunter an die Seiten eines Schreibheftes denken lassen und so Entschlüsseln und Übersetzen als Prozesse nahelegen, die zwangsläufig mit dem Ausdruck von Gefühlen einhergehen. In einer Verneinung textbasierten Wissens schwebt über dem Gehirn ein leeres Buch. Retortengefäße sind den Lungen zur Seite gestellt, um deren reinigende, filtrierende Funktion hervorzuheben. Gemeinsam unterstreichen diese Schlüsselbilder das Moment der Performance, des körperlichen Vorgangs oder auch der „Verarbeitung". Irgendwo findet sich ein Teil eines Gesichts, eine schematische Darstellung aus einem Schulbuch zur Sprachproduktion. Sie zeigt, dass Sprachlaute

For Danz this "illegibilty" of the cube is both intentional and essential. Failure, breakdown as well as the frustration of miscommunication is a central problem of *Cube Cell Stage* and of Danz' work as a whole. Addressing the imposition of language or information structures as colonial practices, in which labeling and definitions become acts of "claiming" authority, Danz repeatedly attempts to break through these processes. This is why she so often draws on methods that operate outside the traditional canon: oral tradition, song, imagery, and, most of all, a leveling and confusion of established orders. As the visuality of the cube indicates, clarity and singularity, linear narrative and coherency are sacrificed in the process. And yet, as the chorus of gesticulating fingers indicates—with an obvious urgency—the cube has something to communicate.

One thing is clear: the body is central to what Danz is trying to tell us. Major internal organs positioned in the middle of each of its four sides seem to serve as touch-keys, central icons made of burnt walnut: the lungs, heart, digestive system, and the brain. Each is activated by the tumbling mass of visual activity surrounding it. On one side, for example, question marks funneled through the stomach and intestine seem to excrete a brain-like, purified white mass. Understanding is apparently a process of digestion. The heart is set in quotation marks with a row of lines below recalling the pages of a ruled notebook and suggesting decipherment and translation as inherent to expressions of emotion. The brain is topped by a book void of text as a negation of text-based knowledge. Test tubes accompany the lungs to underscore their purifying, filtering function. All of these key images further underscore an element of performance, of physical process, or "processing." Somewhere else we find a section of a face, a diagram from a textbook on the production of speech. It illustrates how sounds stem not just from the lips but also the nose and head. Not only "knowing" but also "intoning" is conveyed as an integrative, bodily act.

Without paralleling the languages of action and script, the cube thus gradually emerges as a non-logical Rosetta stone[1] for mediating between the intuitions of the body and the tools of communication, between the physical apparatus and comprehension, between gesture and formal structures of language. It is clear that Danz' challenge to established authorities of information and learning also asserts a rethinking of body as a carrier and mediator of knowledge. René Descartes' famous illustration of the mind/body problem has been delicately painted on one of the panels as a fundamental reference to the complex of questions that preoccupy the artist. Where is the true seat of the brain? Does mind hold sway over matter?

nicht nur mit den Lippen gebildet werden, sondern auch in der Nase und dem Kopf entstehen. Damit wird nicht nur „Wissen", sondern auch „Artikulation" als ein integrativer körperlicher Akt vermittelt.

Ohne die Ausdrucksweisen von Handlung und Schrift gleichzusetzen, tritt der Würfel somit allmählich als ein nicht-logischer „Stein von Rosette"[1] hervor, um zwischen körperlichen Intuitionen und Kommunikationswerkzeugen zu vermitteln, zwischen physischer Apparatur und Verstehen, zwischen Gestik und formalen Sprachstrukturen. Es wird deutlich, dass Danz mit ihrer Infragestellung der etablierten Informations- und Lernautoritäten auch ein Neudenken des Körpers als Träger und Vermittler von Wissen vorstellt. René Descartes' berühmte Illustration des Körper-Geist-Problems ist zart auf eine der Tafeln gemalt, ein wesentlicher Verweis auf den Fragenkomplex, der die Künstlerin beschäftigt. Wo befindet sich der wahre Sitz des Denkens? Herrscht der Geist über die Materie? Wie manifestiert sich Verständnis? Gibt es eine Physiologie des Verstehens? Oder, in den Worten der Künstlerin: „How to know?" – „Wie können wir etwas wissen?"[2] Mit ihrer Behauptung, es gelte, den Körper jenseits des Dualismus von Materialität und Immaterialität zu verstehen, wagt sich Danz in Gebiete vor, die Neurobiolog/innen, Soziobiolog/innen, Evolutionspsycholog/innen, Biosemiotiker/innen und Kognitionswissenschaftler/innen weiterhin viele Fragen aufgeben.

Ungeachtet der gewaltigen Dimension dieses theoretischen Komplexes, den sie sich vorgenommen hat, bleibt Danz unbeirrt bei ihrem Verständnis, dass selbst die hoch gelobten Disziplinen der Wissenschaft auf Traditionen aufbauen, die so wenig vollkommen wie beständig sind. Diese Erkenntnis stammt nicht nur aus ihrem eingehenden Studium der Anatomiegeschichte, sondern auch aus einer intensiven Auseinandersetzung mit Theorien über Subalternität, einer Position, die zwischen kolonialer Autorität und Kolonisierten, zwischen Ermächtigten und Unterworfenen sowie zwischen Konformität und Andersartigkeit vermittelt. Das Hauptanliegen der Künstlerin Danz – ausgedrückt im Kubus – ist die Vermittlung von Fragen der Innerlichkeit und der Kommunikation, und zwar über das Medium Körper, durch Visualisierung und Performance. Außerdem interessiert sich Danz für den Körper als Träger und Behältnis kultureller Bedeutung, für den Moment, in dem nicht nur der Wille des Einzelnen sichtbar wird, sondern auch die Traditionen, die sich im kulturellen Einverständnis gebildet haben. Als Darstellungen von additiven und subtraktiven, zeitgenössischen und historischen Dekonstruktionen des Körpers, stehen sich in den oberen Ecken der

How is comprehension embodied? Is there a physiology of understanding? Or in the artist's own words, "How to know?".[2] In her contention that the body must be understood beyond the dualism of the material and the immaterial, Danz ventures into territory that continues to pose innumerable questions for neuroscientists, sociobiologists, evolutionary psychologists, biosemioticians, and cognitive scientists.

Despite the immensity of the theoretical complex that she has taken on, Danz remains undaunted in her understanding that even the most vaunted fields of science are founded on traditions that are as imperfect as they are impermanent. These realizations draw not only from her intensive research into the history of anatomy but also from a deep engagement with theories of the subaltern, a position mediating between colonial authority and the colonized, the empowered and the subjugated, and between conformity and otherness. As an artist, Danz' main concern, expressed in the cube, is conveying questions of interiority vs. communication through the medium of the body, through visualization and performance. Also, Danz is interested in the body as a carrier and container of cultural meaning, the point where not merely individual volition is manifested but also the traditions formed by cultural agreement. On the panel with the heart two human busts confront each other from the opposite upper corners—an angular "avatar" used for constructing facial features in 3D renderings and a Renaissance anatomical drawing of face stripped to the musculature—as representing additive and subtractive, contemporary and historical deconstructions of the body. Emphasis is placed on the eye of each face, and their reciprocal gaze is marked by a row of tears. Knowing thus seemed inextricably linked with how we see, how we categorize, how we divide and take apart.

Although the cube can be opened, the inside offers no further explanation of the associative order on its exterior. Despite its definite shape and dimensions, the cube is ultimately a flexible structure with endless permutations. It is a nexus of the dialogical push and pull of the affirmations and negations that cut across *Cube Cell Stage*, a model, a unit of bodily proportions that can be spanned, or embraced, by one's outstretched arms, a cell. As a performative space, both for the artist/actor and for the viewer/viewing process, it is intrinsically propositional in character. This is mirrored in a certain erraticism of style—imagery ranging from simple child-like outlines, to tactile moldings and careful renderings. Topped by blue sky and clouds painted on the upper panel, it has an openness even when closed, with the celestial image based on an early computer desktop motif suggesting the unlimited possibilities and radical transformations of our contemporary structures of

Tafel mit dem Herz zwei menschliche Büsten gegenüber: ein kantiger „Avatar" zur Modellierung von Gesichtszügen in 3D und ein anatomisch gezeichnetes Gesicht im Renaissance-Stil, dessen Muskulatur offen liegt. Die Betonung liegt auf den Augen dieser Gesichter; ihr Blickaustausch wird von einer Reihe von Tränen gekennzeichnet. Wissen scheint untrennbar damit verbunden zu sein, wie wir sehen, kategorisieren, abgrenzen und zerlegen.

Der Würfel lässt sich öffnen, doch Erklärungen über die assoziative Ordnung seiner Außenflächen bietet sein Inneres nicht. Trotz der eindeutigen Form und Maße bleibt der Kubus letztlich eine flexible Struktur mit endlosen Variationsmöglichkeiten. Im dialogischen Hin und Her der Bestätigungen und Verneinungen, die *Cube Cell Stage* durchdringen, ist er ein Knotenpunkt, ein Modell, eine Einheit mit körperlichen Proportionen, die man umspannen oder mit gestreckten Armen umfassen kann, eine Zelle. Als ein performativer Raum für die Künstlerin bzw. Akteurin und gleichermaßen für die Betrachter/innen bzw. den Prozess des Zuschauens, hat er naturgemäß einen Aussagecharakter. Dem steht als Spiegelbild eine gewisse stilistische Sprunghaftigkeit gegenüber: Die Bildsprache reicht von der einfachen, kindlichen Umrisszeichnung bis hin zum haptisch wahrnehmbaren Relief und zu fein gearbeiteten Darstellungen. Durch den blauen Himmel mit Wolken auf der oberen Tafel besitzt der Würfel eine Offenheit, selbst wenn er geschlossen ist. Das Himmelsbild geht auf ein frühes Desktopmotiv zurück und verweist so auf die unbegrenzten Möglichkeiten und radikalen Veränderungen unserer zeitgenössischen Wissensstrukturen. So projiziert der Kubus auch vergangene Dynamiken in die Zukunft. Welche Fragmente werden wir mitnehmen, während wir immer weiter ins Paradigma des digitalen Zeitalters vordringen? Welche Autoritäten werden in den Bits und Bytes des aufkommenden Kanons etabliert?

1 Der „Stein von Rosette" ist eine Inschriftstafel aus dem 2. Jahrhundert v. Chr., in die eine Ehrung des ägyptischen Königs Ptolemaios V. in drei Schriften (Altgriechisch, Demotisch, Hieroglyphen) eingemeißelt wurde. Ihre Entdeckung 1799 trug maßgeblich zur Übersetzung der ägyptischen Hieroglyphen bei. Sie befindet sich heute im British Museum, London.

2 *How to know*, UNMAP 2011.

knowledge. Thus, the cube also projects the dynamics of the past into the future. Advancing further into the paradigm of the digital age, what fragments will we carry with us? What authorities will be asserted within the bits and bytes of the next emerging canon?

1 The Rosetta Stone is an inscription dating from the 2nd century B.C., which bears a text honoring the Egyptian King Ptolemy V in three languages (ancient Greek, Demotic, and Hieroglyphics). Its discovery in 1799 was crucial to the decipherment of Egyptian Hieroglyphics. Today the Rosetta Stone is in the collection of the British Museum, London.

2 *How to know*, UNMAP 2011.

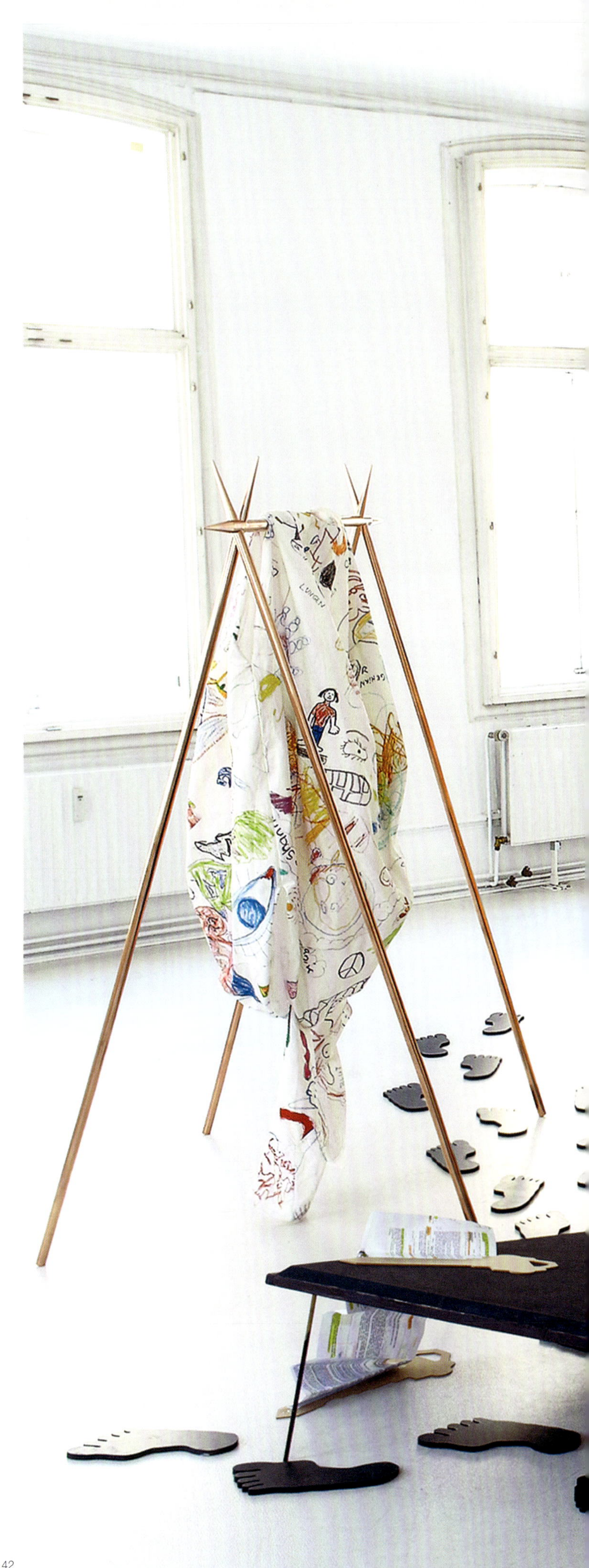

Installation view *Cube Cell Stage*, Kunstverein Göttingen.

Page 44: *Body/ydob, a flayed mirage* (detail), 2012.

Page 45: *Body/ydob, a flayed mirage*, 2012.

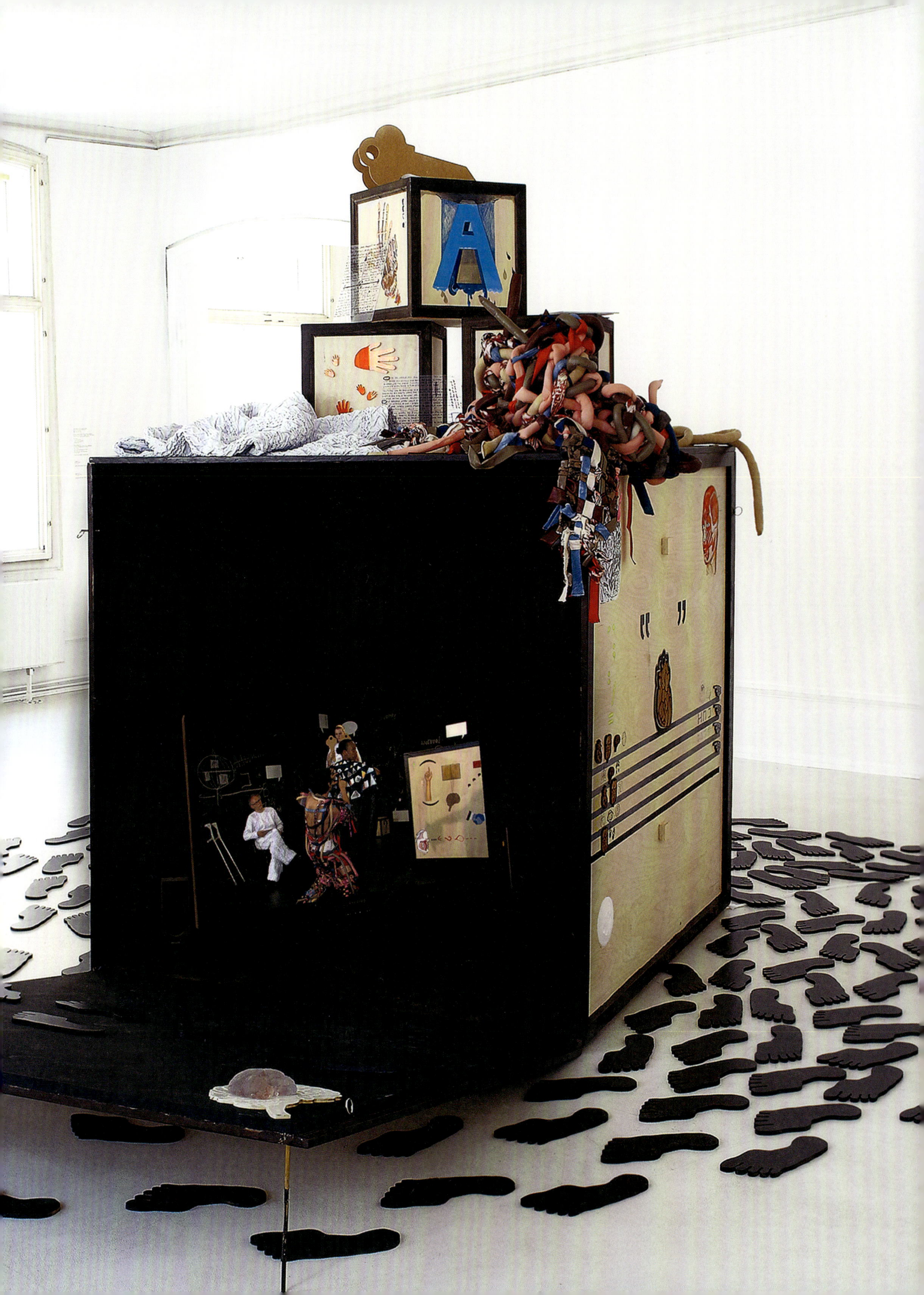

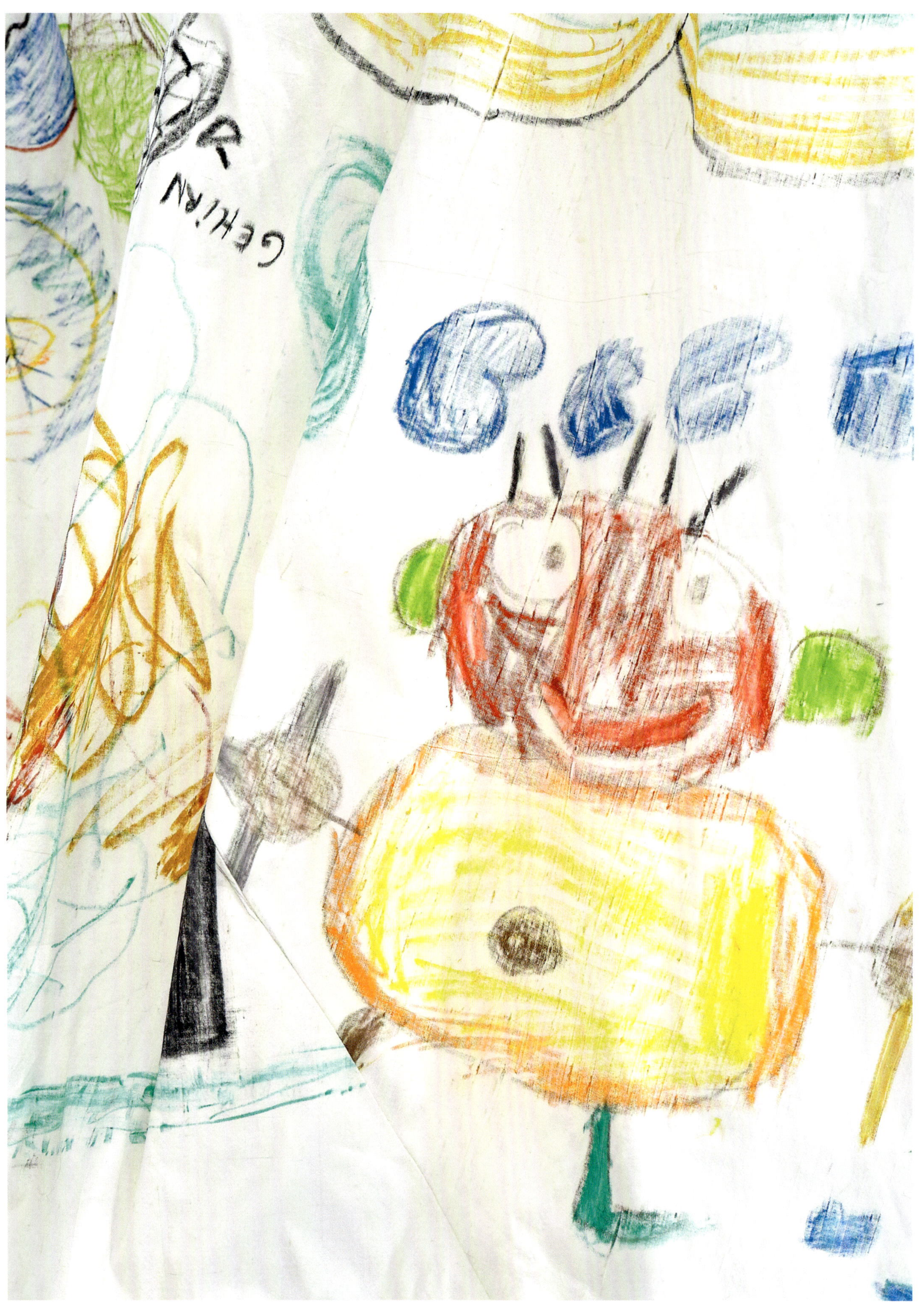
GEHIRN

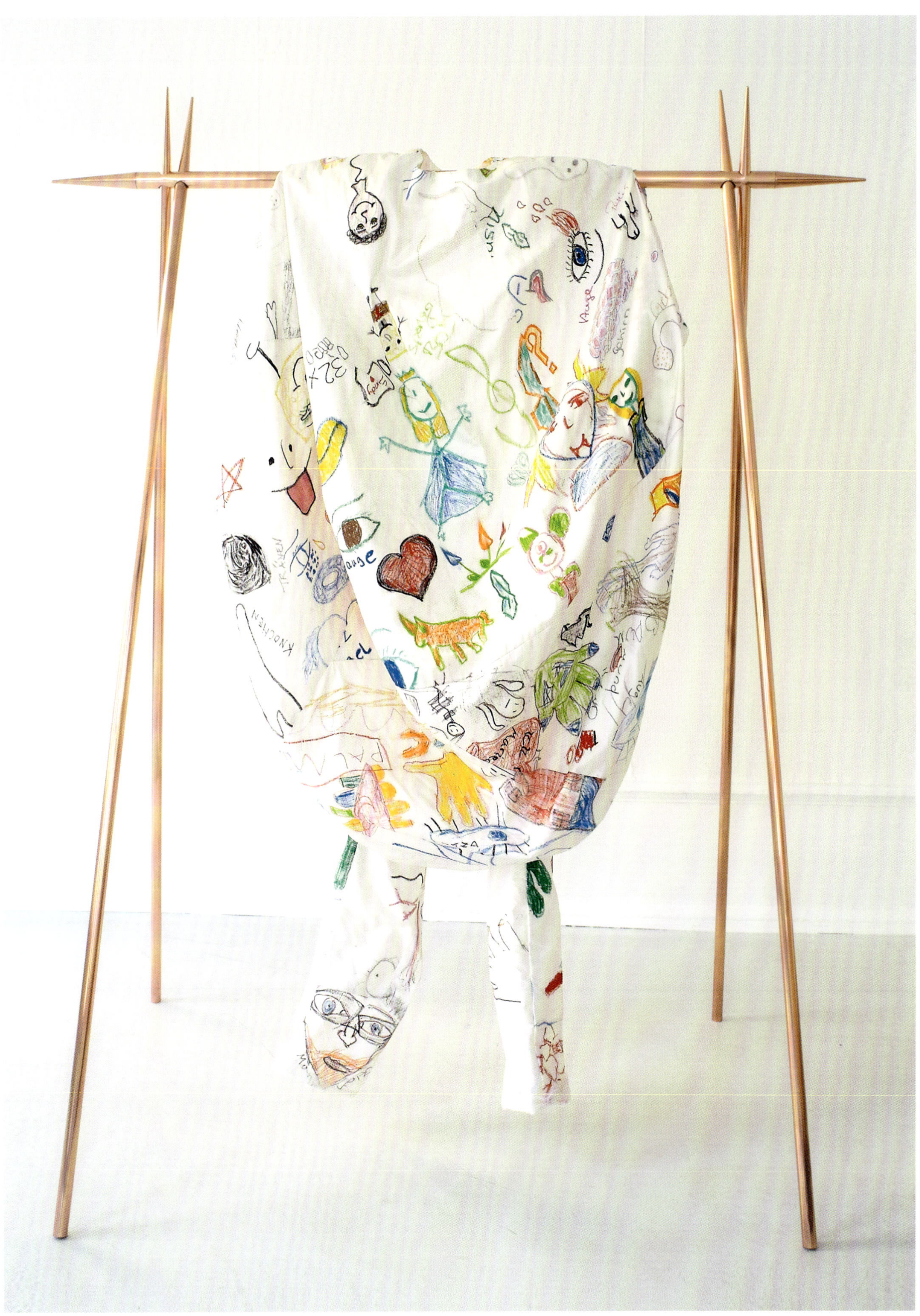
Auge
KNOCHEN

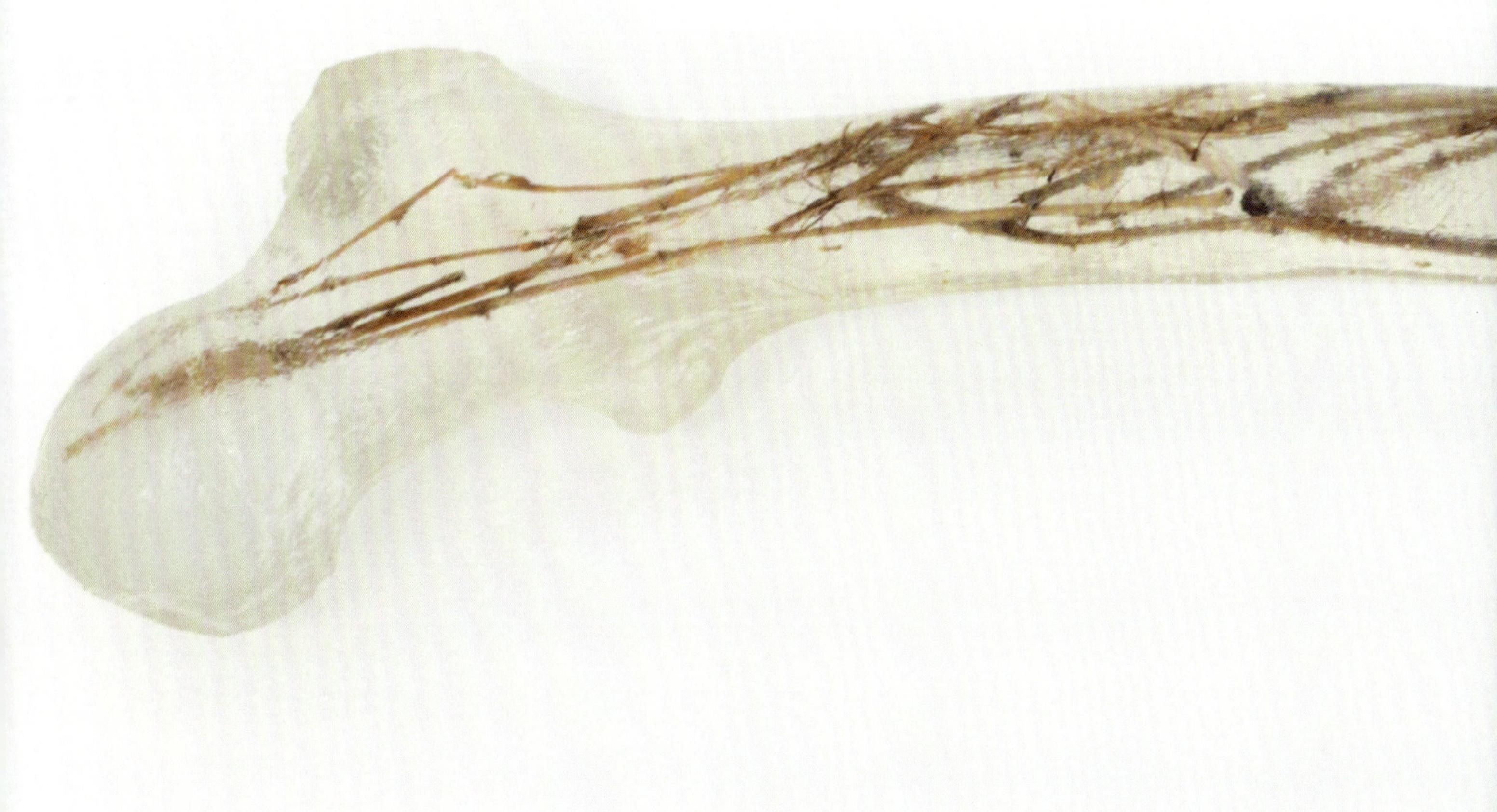

Soil Sample Organ (Bone), 2011.

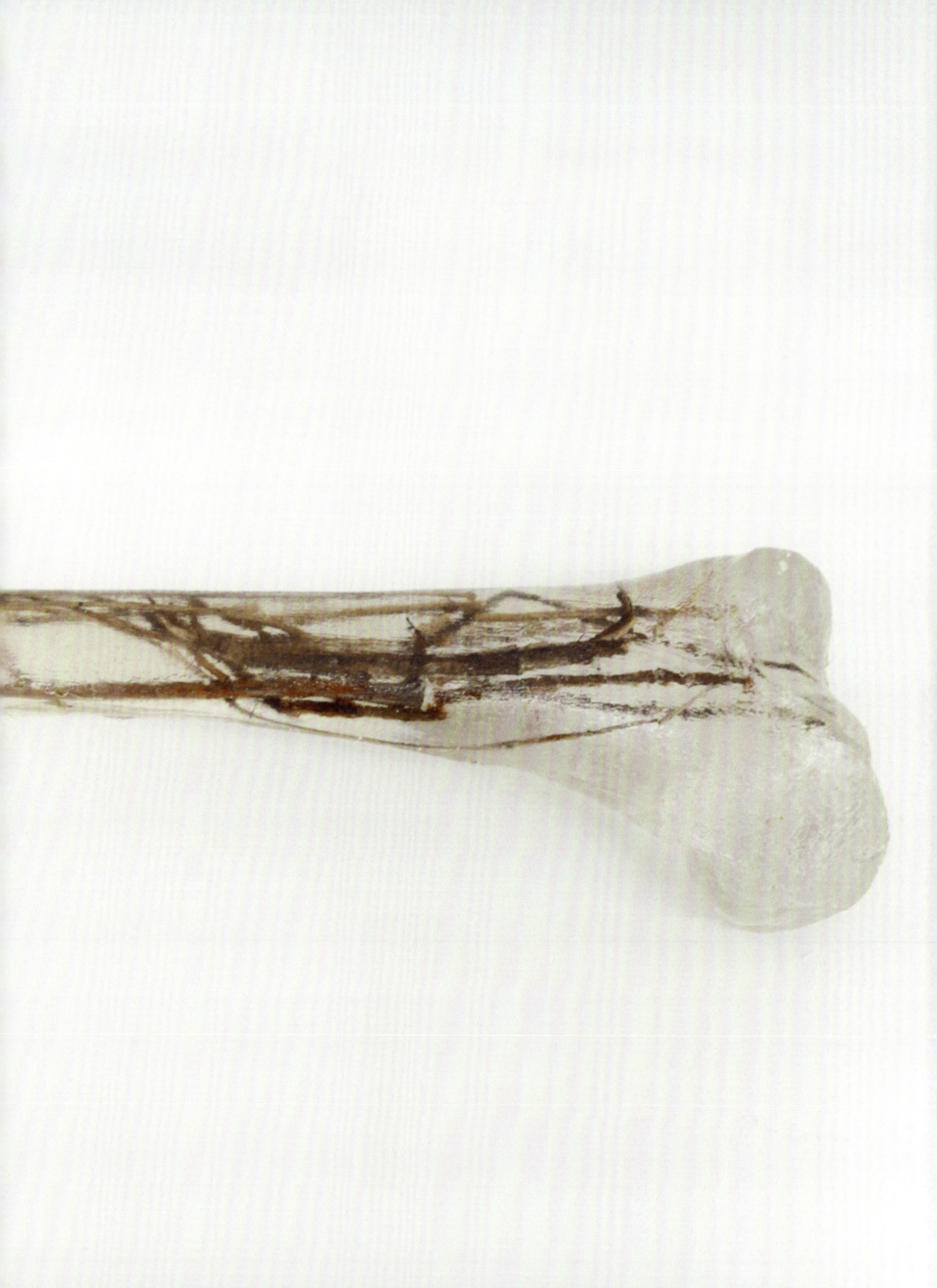

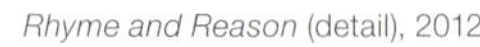

Rhyme and Reason (detail), 2012.

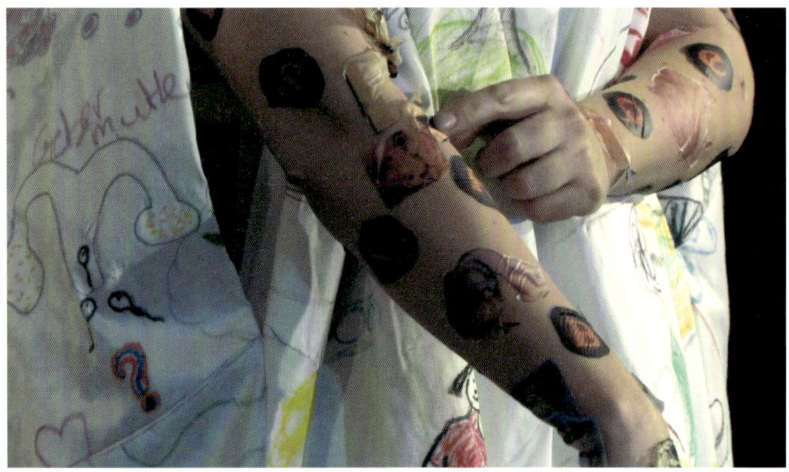

CUBE, CELL, STAGE, ODER: WIE VERLEIBT MAN SICH EINE BIBLIOTHEK EIN?[1]

CUBE, CELL, STAGE, OR: HOW DO WE INTERNALIZE A LIBRARY?[1]

VALERIE SMITH

So wie ein Würfel – die vollkommenste Form des positivistischen Denkens – eine vom Menschen künstlich geschaffene Form mit festgelegten Maßen ist, so handelt es sich bei der Zelle um den Kern des Lebens, sieht man einmal von der Idee der Vollkommenheit als natürlicher Quelle zahlreicher Widersprüche ab. Diese beiden Elemente bilden die Bühne für einen Wettstreit zwischen allem, was zu wissen möglich ist, und allem, was sich nicht wissen lässt. Mit dieser Versuchsanordnung konfrontiert uns Mariechen Danz in einer Reihe audiovisueller Performances, die ihrem persönlichen „stream of consciousness" folgen.

Betritt man Danz' theatralischen Raum im Kunstverein Göttingen, so fühlt man sich wie Alice im Wunderland unweigerlich von dessen sonderbarer Verspieltheit angezogen. In nicht-hierarchischer Anordnung wurden auf die Seitenflächen eines riesigen Würfels menschliche Organe gemalt, geklebt und reliefartig aufgebracht, die eine hieroglyphenartige Wirkung erzeugen. Hinweisende Finger lenken den Blick in konkurrierende Richtungen durch dicht gedrängte grammatische Codes und Symbole und jene rastlose Fülle versprengter anatomischer Fragmente, die jede der quadratischen Flächen bedecken. Kleinere Lernkuben mit Buchstaben und anderen Zeichen krönen den gigantischen Würfel inmitten eines Gewirrs aus gedärmartigen, ausgestopften Schläuchen und anderen Kostümen, die von seiner festlich geschmückten Oberseite ausgehen. Ein großer Schlüssel, der den oberen Abschluss der gesamten Würfelkonstruktion bildet, verwandelt sich in ein Faltmenü: Er „öffnet nichts und öffnet etwas Eingeschlossenes", heißt es in der auf Video dokumentierten Performance[2] – hier vermittelt sich der Geist der Organe, der aus dem Inneren des Würfels ertönt.

Just as a cube—the quintessential form of positivist thought—is a man-made form of certain and perfect measurements; so the cell is the nucleus of life, beyond the concept of perfection, a natural host of contradictions. These two elements set the stage for a duel between all that is knowable and all that is not. Such is the conundrum that Mariechen Danz places before us in a series of audio and visual events along her stream of consciousness.

Entering Danz' theatrical space at the Kunstverein Göttingen we feel drawn to its curious playfulness as Alice was in Wonderland. In a non-hierarchical arrangement, body parts are painted, sculpted and pasted onto the sides of a giant cube to hieroglyphic effect. Grammatical codes and symbols pressed along by pointing fingers pull the eye in competing directions through a restless profusion of anatomical fragments that flash and float on each square surface. Smaller learning blocks with alphabets and other signs crown the large cube amidst a tumbling nest of intestine-like stuffed tubes and other colorful costumes protruding off its festive top. A large key, which caps the entire cubic construction, transforms into an accordion-like menu. It "opens nothing and opens something locked," so we learn from the performance documented as a video[2]—a mediated organ-spirit that sounds off from inside the cube.

What can this assembly of things be other than the tools for an epic drama on the origin of knowledge? Indeed, in her performance *Rhyme and Reason,* which took place at GAK Gesellschaft für Aktuelle Kunst Bremen, Danz animates the language of signs and symbols with the assistance of three other performers. They are all vested in jumpsuits, some

Was könnte diese Ansammlung von Dingen wohl anderes sein als die Requisiten eines epischen Dramas über den Ursprung des Wissens? Tatsächlich haucht Danz in ihrer Performance *Rhyme and Reason*, die in der GAK Gesellschaft für Aktuelle Kunst Bremen stattfand, der Sprache aus Zeichen und Symbolen mit Hilfe dreier weiterer Darsteller/innen Leben ein. Sie alle tragen Overalls, die zum Teil mit Körperteilen und mit verbildlichten Pyramiden von Stufenkategorien versehen sind. Zusammen beherrschen sie in ihren wechselnden professoralen, linguistischen und musikalischen Rollen die vier Ecken des Würfels.

Dieses kubische Monument des Lernens ist rundum von einer durchgehenden Wandtafel umgeben, auf der Sprechblasen angebracht sind und die, wie im Video zu sehen ist, für die schulartigen Demonstrationen und pädagogischen Graffitis der Akteure innerhalb der Installation genutzt wird. Die hier vermittelten Informationen sind rational, ja mathematisch, während die Darbietung der Performer/innen autoritär wirkt und zuweilen ans Absurde grenzt. Eine einzelne Performance-Sequenz beginnt unter Umständen mit einer Aussage über das Reden als Ursprung der Sprache im Körper. Daraus ergeben sich im Folgenden Klänge von Konsonanten, die optisch vom Torso über den Mund auf die Tafel projiziert werden und schließlich in einer plötzlich ertönenden, harmonischen Melodie lyrische Gestalt annehmen. Man fühlt sich an Filmmusicals erinnert, in denen sich emotionale Themen in Liedern entladen und zu enthusiastischen Erkenntnismomenten aufschwingen.

Der Tenor von *Rhyme and Reason* wird allein erzeugt durch die transformative Kraft der Anatomie, welche in Danz' Objekten, Zeichnungen und Kostümen der Vermittlung von Konzeption und Ausarbeitung eines allgemeinen Entwurfs der Aneignung von Wissen dient. Dabei entsteht der Eindruck, dass diese Dinge nur dazu geschaffen wurden, um das Schauspiel in Gang zu setzen. Letztlich jedoch führen sie eine eigenständige Existenz im Sinne erstarrter Elemente innerhalb einer gewissermaßen bewohnten Installation, einer Art Labor mit all seinen dazugehörigen Komponenten, aufgrund derer wir diese Kunst schnell als prozessorientiert kategorisieren. Danz verdeutlicht in *Cube Cell Stage* den Sachverhalt, ohne ihn ausdrücklich zu formulieren: Alles ist ein Prozess des Hinzufügens oder Subtrahierens, des Aufbauens oder Zerstörens, sei es nun bei der Herstellung einer Skulptur, einer Zeichnung oder einer Bühne, auf der sich eine bestimmte chemische Reaktion ereignen soll.

In den Arbeiten von Mariechen Danz wird die syntaktische Geste, die verschiedene Aspekte ihres Werks miteinander

emblazoned with body parts and image pyramids of tiered categories. Together they command the four corners of the cube in alternating professorial, linguistic, and musical roles.

This cubical monument to learning is surrounded by a continuous chalkboard punctuated by speech bubbles, which, as seen on video, serviced the classroom-like demonstrations and pedagogic graffiti of the players inside the exhibition. The information is rational even mathematical. The performers' delivery is imperial, bordering on the absurd. A performance sequence might begin with a statement on the origin of language in the body through speech. It evolves into sounds of consonants physically projected from the torso up through the mouth onto the chalkboard and finally, taking shape as poetry in a burst of harmonic melody. I am reminded of film musicals, in which emotional themes erupt into song, soaring into elated moments of recognition.

The thrust of *Rhyme and Reason* is solidly held by the transformative power of anatomy, supported by Danz' objects, drawings, and costumes, to convey the concept and design of a broader project on knowledge acquisition. There is a sense that these things are created to drive the drama. Yet, at the end of the day, they exist on their own: frozen elements of a lived-in installation, a laboratory of sorts with all its requisite components for what we are quick to categorize as a process-oriented art. Danz' *Cube Cell Stage* makes it clear without having to spell it out: everything is a process of adding and subtracting, constructing or destroying whether it be in order to make a sculpture, a drawing, or to build a stage for a certain chemistry to take place.

Throughout her work, hands in various material representations manipulate the syntactical gesture that binds different sections of her work together. They recur in her Kunstverein Göttingen exhibition, as do feet prints that circle the cube, like traces of a pilgrim's tour around the Kaaba. Intestines, hearts, and brains appropriated across historical and cultural lines also abound in objects, which then become the basic starting points for language and information in the performance. Like some available primordial material, the body is called up to perform the rhythmic sounds that may begin with the pronouncement of the consonant "b" and eventually evolve into emotive words like "breath" and "breast" used for their etymological connection to food, language, and nurturing. Here, memory is tied to cultural understanding in a physical way just like breathing in is contingent on breathing out, which also mimics the hydraulic system of the heart, and so on. These repetitive binary mechanisms play in the cadence

verbindet, mit Hilfe von in verschiedenen Materialien realisierten Abbildungen von Händen manifest. Diese tauchen in ihrer Ausstellung im Kunstverein Göttingen ebenso auf wie Fußabdrücke, die kreisförmig um den Würfel herumführen wie die Spuren der Pilger rund um die Kaaba. Die über historische und kulturelle Grenzen hinweg miteinander kombinierten Darstellungen von Därmen, Herzen und Gehirnen wimmeln außerdem von Objekten, die ihrerseits im Rahmen der Performance als Ausgangspunkte für Sprache und Informationen dienen. Als zur Verfügung stehendes Urmaterial ist der Körper aufgerufen, jene rhythmischen Geräusche hervorzubringen, die beispielsweise mit der Artikulation des Konsonanten „b" beginnen und schließlich so emotional aufgeladene Wörter wie „breath" und „breast" ergeben, die Danz aufgrund ihrer etymologischen Verbindung zu Ernährung, Sprache und körperlicher Pflege auswählte. An diesem Punkt ist Erinnerung in derselben leiblichen Weise an ein kulturelles Verständnis gebunden, wie das Einatmen mit dem Ausatmen zusammenhängt, worin sich auch das hydraulische System des Herzens widerspiegelt und so weiter. Diese repetitiven binären Mechanismen spielen im gleichen Takt der Performance und der künstlerischen Objekte innerhalb der Installation, der komplexen Zeichnungen und der vielfältigen anatomischen und linguistischen Diagramme, die weniger der Wissensvermittlung als der Forschung dienen. Dies belegt auch der Text, den Danz in *Rhyme and Reason* singt:

„Write a word,
A mark, a learning,
To illustrate how
Language is searching.
Point on map
A mark, a learning,
To relocate where
Borders are merging.
Who's nursing?
Or operating?

No memory.
No learning.
A key."[3]

An einer späteren Stelle des Videos von der Performance sieht man, wie sich auf der Wandtafel die Bedeutungen unterschiedlicher Formen geschriebener Sprache herausbilden. So spiegeln sich in den als Lektion auf den Würfeln und der Skulptur-Haut von *Common Carrier Case* ausgeschriebenen lateinischen, chinesischen und ägyptischen Buchstaben beziehungsweise Schriftzeichen ihre ungefähren bildlichen

of the performance and the artworks within the installation, with their elaborate drawings, project multifaceted anatomic and linguistic maps created less to teach than to explore. This bears out in Danz' lyrics sung in *Rhyme and Reason*:

"Write a word,
A mark, a learning,
To illustrate how
Language is searching.
Point on map
A mark, a learning,
To relocate where
Borders are merging.
Who's nursing?
Or operating?

No memory.
No learning.
A key."[3]

Further along in the video of the performance, we watch the meanings of multiple written language forms evolve on the chalkboard. For example, Latin, Chinese, and Egyptian letters written out as a lesson action reverberate with their approximate pictorial equivalents on the cubes and the sculptural skins of the *Common Carrier Cases*. Hi-tech digital renderings of heads and bodies inhabit the same reality as a 15th century Vein Man from Iran and an ivory anatomical figure from the Renaissance (see: *Tower Vessel Tooth*, 2010). Iconographies and alphabets brook no hierarchical categories imposed by external forces, but exist in equal importance in the field of world edification. As viewers, we become acutely aware how language differences can morph into each other, collapsing an individual cultural meaning into an extended family tree of shared meanings and comprehension. It is the cultural and the geographical differences—the sum of multifarious interpretations over time, space, and through other eyes and literacies—that builds knowledge and allows language to be a living and moving thing.

Danz follows in the formidable tradition of contemporary artists, such as John Bock and Mike Kelley, whose performances are the mainstay of their practice. She retains a similar elementary grade-school style about *Rhyme and Reason* that probes, yet without the showy irony, masculine self-mockery and personal deprecation of these precedents. Her work does not explicitly revel in the scatological atmosphere of the carnavalesque. It is rather propelled by

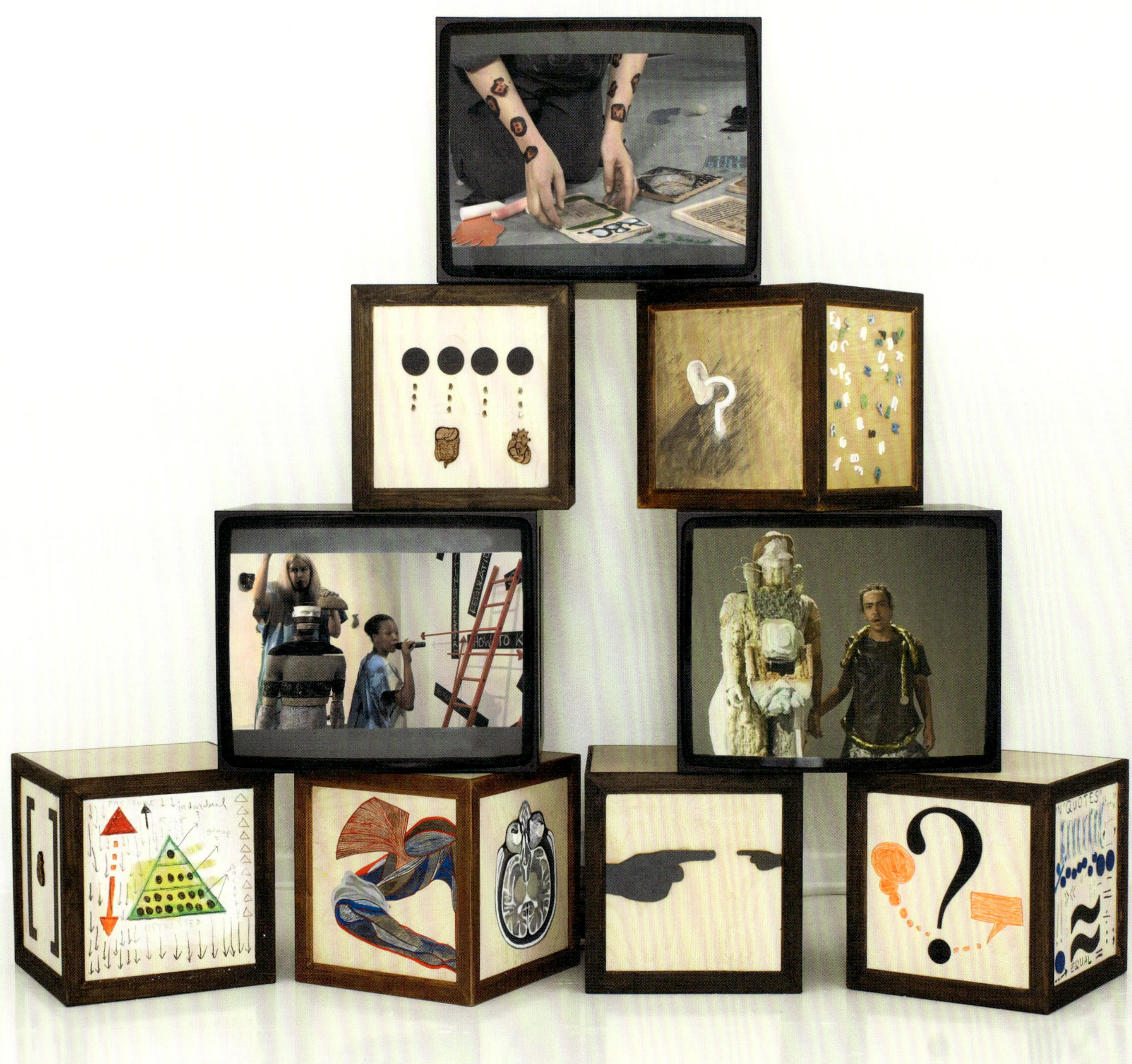

Learning Cubes TV Tower, 2012.

Right: *un un learning*, 2011; *Complain the Explanation*, 2008; *Knot in Arrow: The Dig of No Body*, 2011 (performance stills).

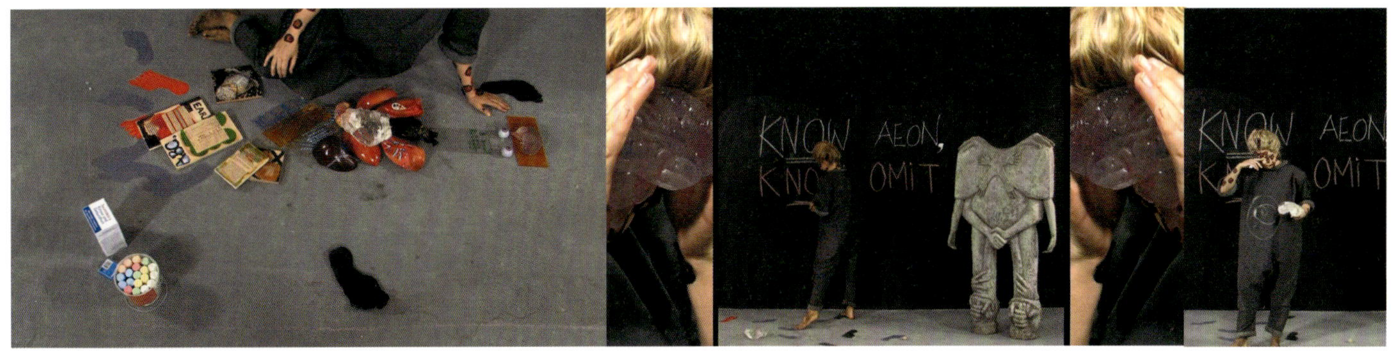
KNOW AEON,
OMIT

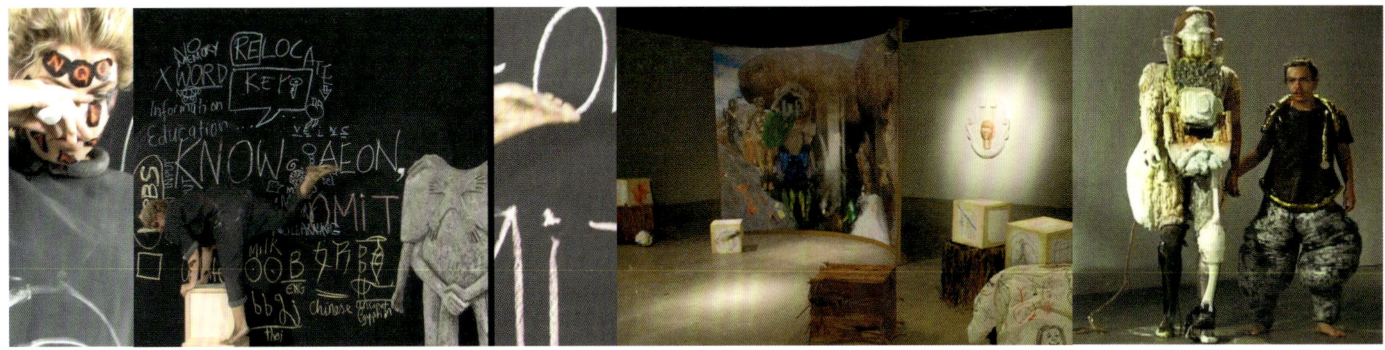
RELOCATE
KEY
Information
Education
KNOW AEON,
OMIT
Chinese

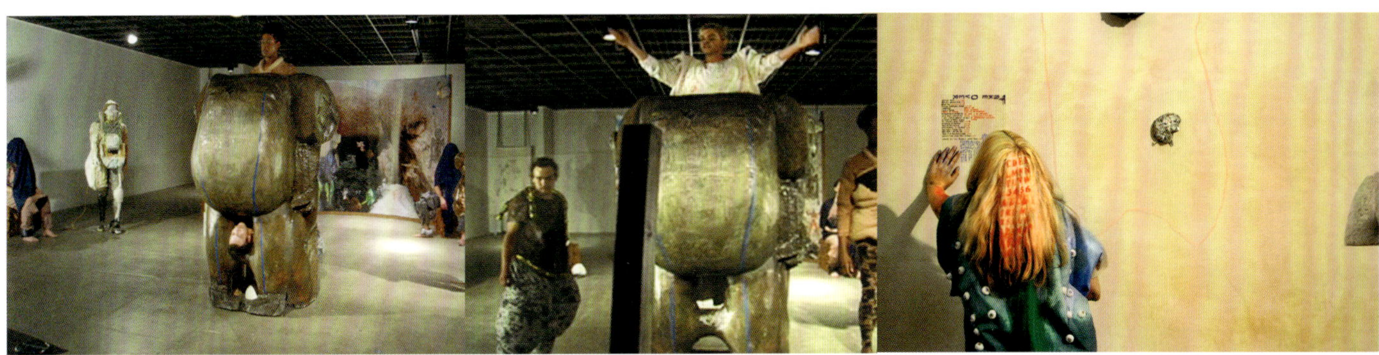

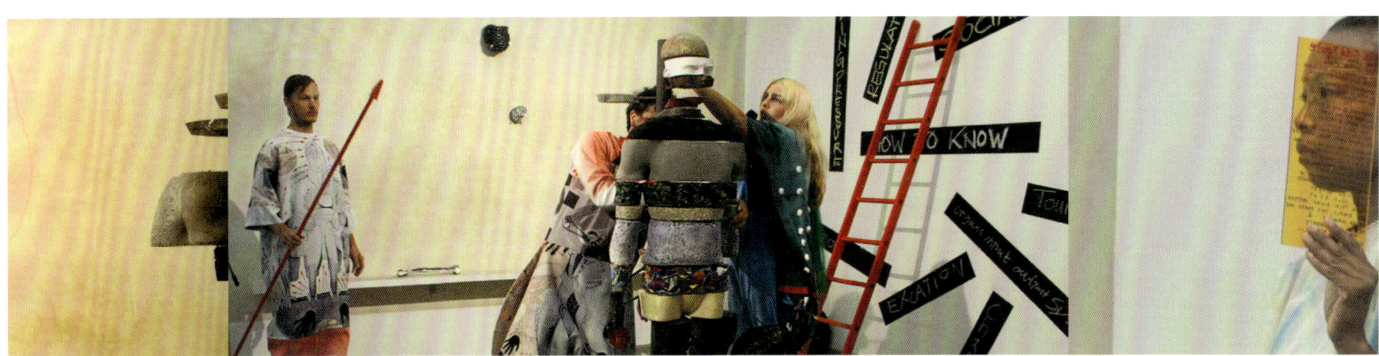
HOW TO KNOW

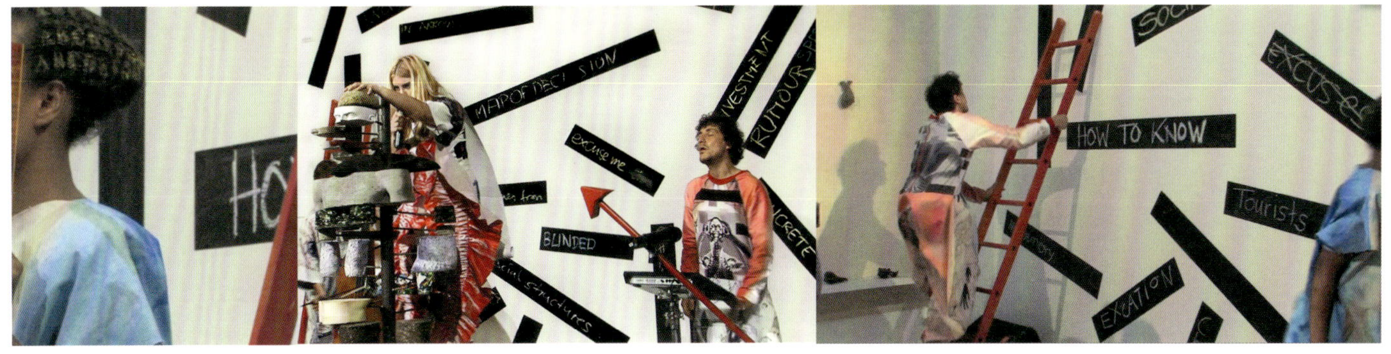
HOW TO KNOW
Tourists
BLINDED
excuse me

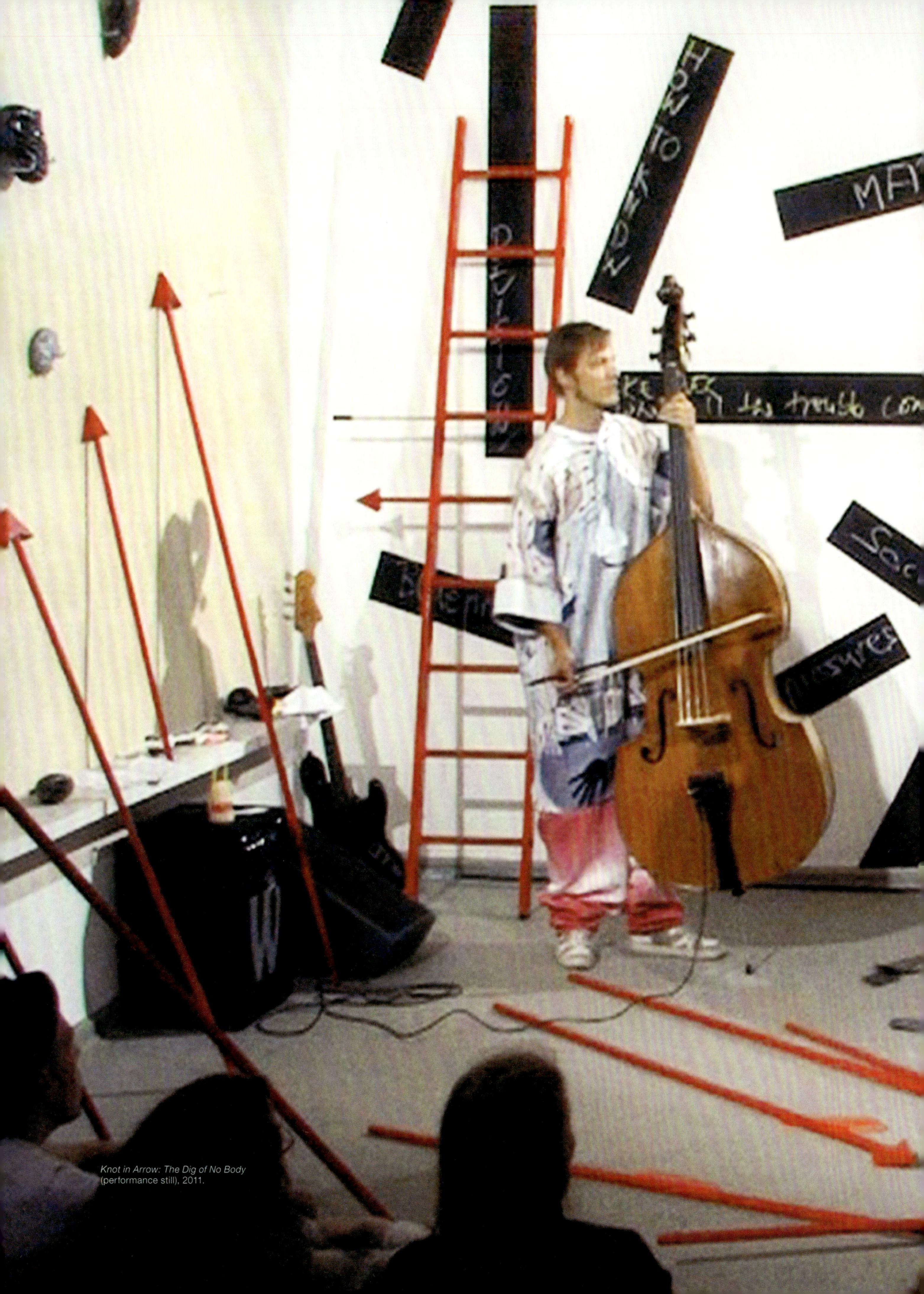

Knot in Arrow: The Dig of No Body
(performance still), 2011.

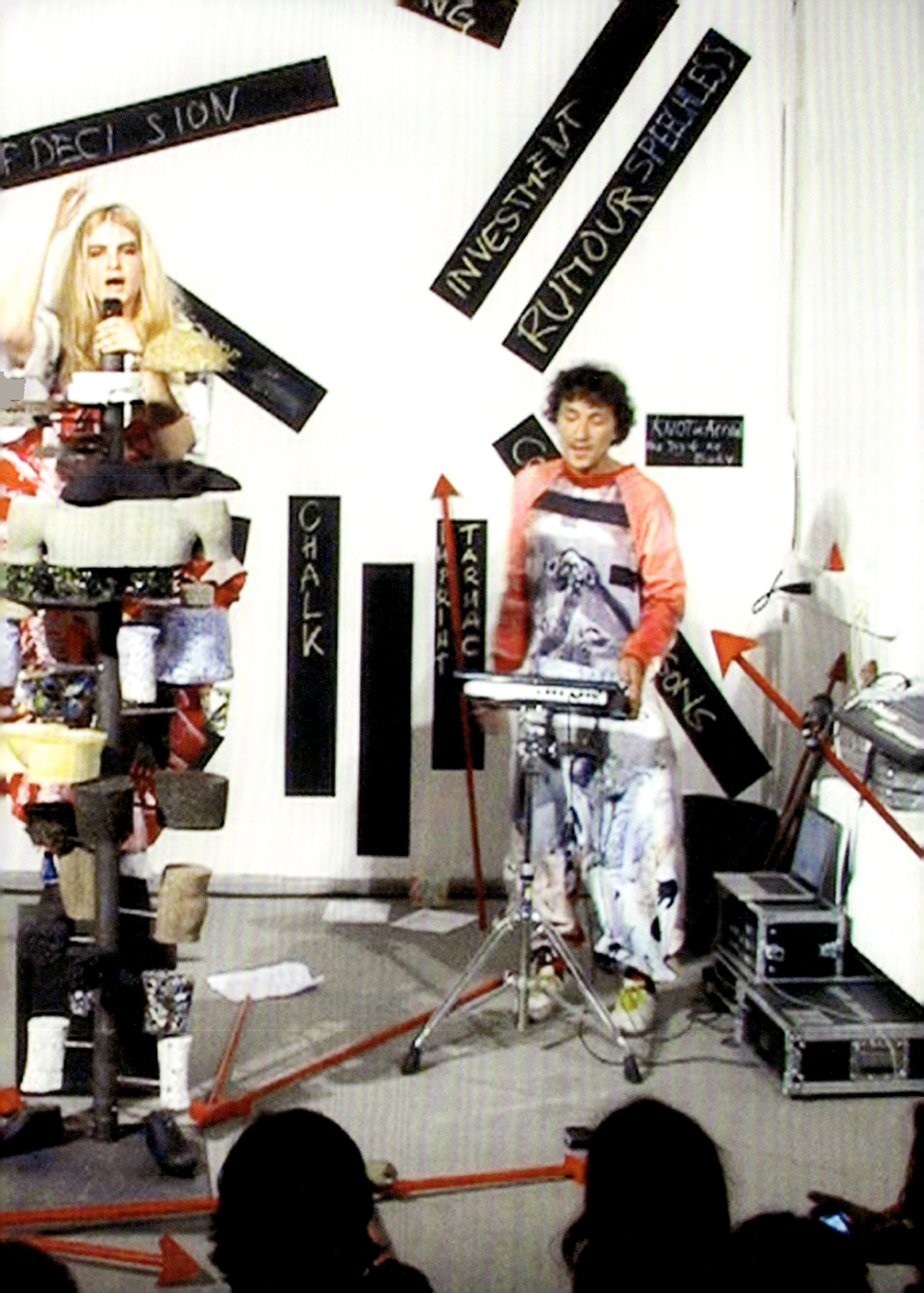
DECI SION
INVESTMENT
RUMOUR SPEECHLESS
CHALK
TARMAC

Entsprechungen wider. Digitale Hightech-Renderings von Köpfen und Körpern teilen dieselbe Realität wie eine Darstellung des menschlichen Blutkreislaufs aus dem Iran des 15. Jahrhunderts oder eine elfenbeinerne anatomische Figur der Renaissance (vgl. *Tower Vessel Tooth*, 2010). Die Ikonografien und Schriftsysteme dulden keine von außen auferlegten, hierarchischen Kategorien, sondern existieren, auf die Schöpfung von Welt bezogen, gleichwertig nebeneinander. Den Betrachter/innen wird unmissverständlich vor Augen geführt, wie Sprachunterschiede ineinander übergehen können, wobei sich eine einzelne kulturelle Bedeutung zu einem ausgedehnten Stammbaum gemeinsamer Bedeutungen und Erkenntnisse verästeln kann. Es sind jene kulturellen und geografischen Unterschiede – die Gesamtheit der vielfältigen, im Laufe der Zeit an verschiedenen Orten und aufgrund eines jeweils eigenen Blickwinkels und Bildungshintergrunds entstandenen Deutungen – durch die Wissen gebildet und Sprache zu etwas Lebendigem und Beweglichem wird.

Danz steht in einer eindrucksvollen Tradition zeitgenössischer Künstler wie John Bock und Mike Kelley, in deren künstlerischer Praxis die Performance eine wesentliche Stütze ist. Sie nutzt bei *Rhyme and Reason* einen ähnlich grundschulartigen, forschenden Stil, wenn auch ohne die zur Schau gestellte Ironie, die männliche Selbstpersiflage und persönliche Geringschätzung ihrer Vorgänger. Ihre Arbeit schwelgt nicht ausdrücklich in der skatologischen Atmosphäre des Karnevalesken, sondern ist vielmehr von dem sehnlichen Wunsch motiviert, die Widersprüche zwischen menschlichem Körper und Geist als Entitäten aufzuzeigen, die von den gesellschaftlichen Gepflogenheiten und ökonomischen Erwartungen des jeweils gegebenen Kontextes geprägt sind. Tritt das Groteske in Erscheinung, beispielsweise in Danz' *Tower Vessel Tooth* und *Common Carrier Cases* – den Kostümen und verschiedenen frühen Zeichnungen von 2006–2012 –, so geschieht dies gleichberechtigt mit allem, was innerhalb der Installation sonst noch vor sich geht, und in offensichtlichem Widerspruch zur banalen Idee des Normalen. Auf diese Weise tarnt sie den unsinnigen Cargo-Kult aus in ihren Arbeiten eingebetteten Referenzen wirksam als technische Anleitung und Gelehrsamkeit.

Die mit verworrenen, Hieronymus-Bosch-artigen Leibern und Innereien oder Kinderzeichnungen verzierten und dick gepolsterten Ganzkörperkostüme tun gut daran, die vertrauten Merkmale eines individuellen menschlichen Körpers zu verbergen. Dadurch übernehmen die von ihrer Identität als reale Menschen in abstrakte Elemente verwandelten Darsteller die Eigenschaften genau jener Subjekte, auf die sie verweisen.

the soulful desire to show up the contradictions of the human body and mind as entities steered by the social customs and economical expectations of any given context. When the grotesque appears, as it does in Danz' *Tower Vessel Tooth* and *Common Carrier Cases*—the costumes and various early drawings from 2006–2012—it is on par with everything else going on in the installation, openly in opposition to some mundane idea of the normal. In this way she effectively clothes the nonsensical cargo culture of references embedded in her artworks in the guise of technical instruction and erudition.

Balloony costumes decorated with Bosch-like confused corpses and innards, or children's pictures do well to obscure the familiar attributes of an individual human body. In this way the players, transformed from their identity as real humans into abstract composites, take on the qualities of the very subjects of which they speak. Does the subject speak from the perspective of the child about the world? Or, as illustrated in the object, *Learning Organ (intestine)*, does it speak from the gut—the intestines? Is information coming from a degreed or authoritative position or an innocent one? Whether empirical or intuitive the overarching question Danz poses is does one think with one's whole body or just a part of it? And from where does one speak and how? Danz performs acts of learning as ways of processing and harnessing the material world. Like this she is able to come to terms with it—control it, give it form.

The question of memory is often evoked in the text of her lyrics and on the walls of her installations. At the first instance we are to understand that profound learning is impossible if it is done by memory, by rote:

"How do we internalize a library?
Memory is not intelligence.
To repeat is not to know.
Comparison isn't reason.
There is the ground and the background."[4]

On the other hand, Danz seems to say that to learn about the meaning of things requires a memory reference before fresh learning can occur. We come with our cultural references a priori to a new learning situation. Certainly, if we agree that the origin of knowledge is a story passed down from generation to generation, the concept of memory becomes a prerequisite to communication. The preconditions for the receptive body is in this way problematized by a desire to shed the entrapment of one's own cultural heritage:

Spricht das Subjekt aus der Perspektive des Kindes über die Welt? Oder, wie im Objekt *Learning Organ (intestine)* veranschaulicht, spricht es aus dem Bauch, den Eingeweiden, heraus? Verdanken sich die jeweiligen Informationen einem Standpunkt der Gelehrsamkeit und Autorität oder einem der Unwissenheit? Ob empirisch oder intuitiv betrachtet, die von Danz formulierte, alles verbindende Frage lautet: Denkt man mit dem ganzen Körper oder nur mit einem Teil desselben? Und von wo aus spricht man überhaupt, und wie? Danz führt Lernakte als Möglichkeiten der Verarbeitung und Nutzbarmachung der materiellen Welt vor. So gelingt es ihr, sich mit ihr zu arrangieren – sie zu beherrschen und ihr eine Gestalt zu verleihen.

In ihren Gesangstexten sowie an den Wänden ihrer Installationen stellt Danz häufig die Frage nach der Erinnerung. Zuallererst müssen wir begreifen, dass fundiertes Lernen unmöglich ist, wenn es auf bloßem Erinnern, also auswendig Gelerntem, basiert:

„How do we internalize a library?
Memory is not intelligence.
To repeat is not to know.
Comparison isn't reason.
There is the ground and the background."[4]

Gleichzeitig scheint sie zu bedenken zu geben, dass zum Erlernen der Bedeutung von Dingen zunächst ein Erinnerungsbezug erforderlich ist, sodass Neues erlernt werden kann. Wir begegnen neuen Lernsituationen aufgrund unserer kulturellen Bezüge a priori. Wenn wir darin übereinstimmen, dass die Quelle des Wissens eine von einer Generation an die nächste weitergegebene Erzählung ist, so wird die Vorstellung von der Erinnerung zu einer Voraussetzung für Kommunikation an sich. Die Grundbedingung für den rezeptiven Körper wird somit durch den Wunsch problematisiert, die Verstrickungen des eigenen kulturellen Erbes abzustreifen:

„Excuse me sir:
Can you speak to me in a language
I don't understand?
No big deal,
It's just that I'm obsessed with
Attempting to establish
Some basic connection
Between BODY, HISTORY, DESTINY,
POLITICS OF LANGUAGE
& psychology."[5]

"Excuse me sir:
Can you speak to me in a language
I don't understand?
No big deal,
It's just that I'm obsessed with
Attempting to establish
Some basic connection
Between BODY, HISTORY, DESTINY,
POLITICS OF LANGUAGE
& psychology."[5]

With this big theme, Danz is sincere in her attempt to create an atmosphere that is open and free, making her position felt in song. The structure of her performance works, like an album of thoughts that confirms our understanding of the world as a constructed one, starts with the collective interpretation of oral histories. "Some say the books inside the chests have begun to talk," quotes Danz from a Mayan proverb, "it is society, not script that determines who can read and in what way can read."

Danz has been involved with performance since graduate school where she elaborated various scenarios that profiled her costumes as if they were living maps. Middle Eastern "coffee house paintings" functioned in much the same way: an itinerant artist travelled from café to café recounting the history of the region through the deeds of its heroes and villains represented in a painting. Rather than canvas and history, Danz prints on cotton fashioned into a type of suit as a surface and a vessel for coded messages, perhaps about the future of humanity. As if guarding the cube and the stage, these two large suits, called *Common Carrier Case (Präparat)*, stoically stand sandwiched behind glass fastened by surrealistic hands and arms casts in green and red epoxy. These sculptures, assuming the role of costumes, are also drawings digitized onto cloth and stuffed to hold a robust position, adopting the atavistic look of armored samurai. On the frontal side one might find the ubiquitous images of intestines, brains or spinal cords merging into one another like grafted flora. On the verso, rubbings of coin heads, the head of Homo erectus, and other bio-figurative composites are advertised. Danz has suggested avatar models, which wear the knowledge of the world like a skin that shields against unforeseen attacks. These anatomically ornamented, yet disembodied suits, are a hybrid of early Japanese manga or current productions of animé, just as much as the studies of physiognomic aberrations, which began with the ancients and lead up to famous 18th century scientists, such as Johann Caspar Lavater.

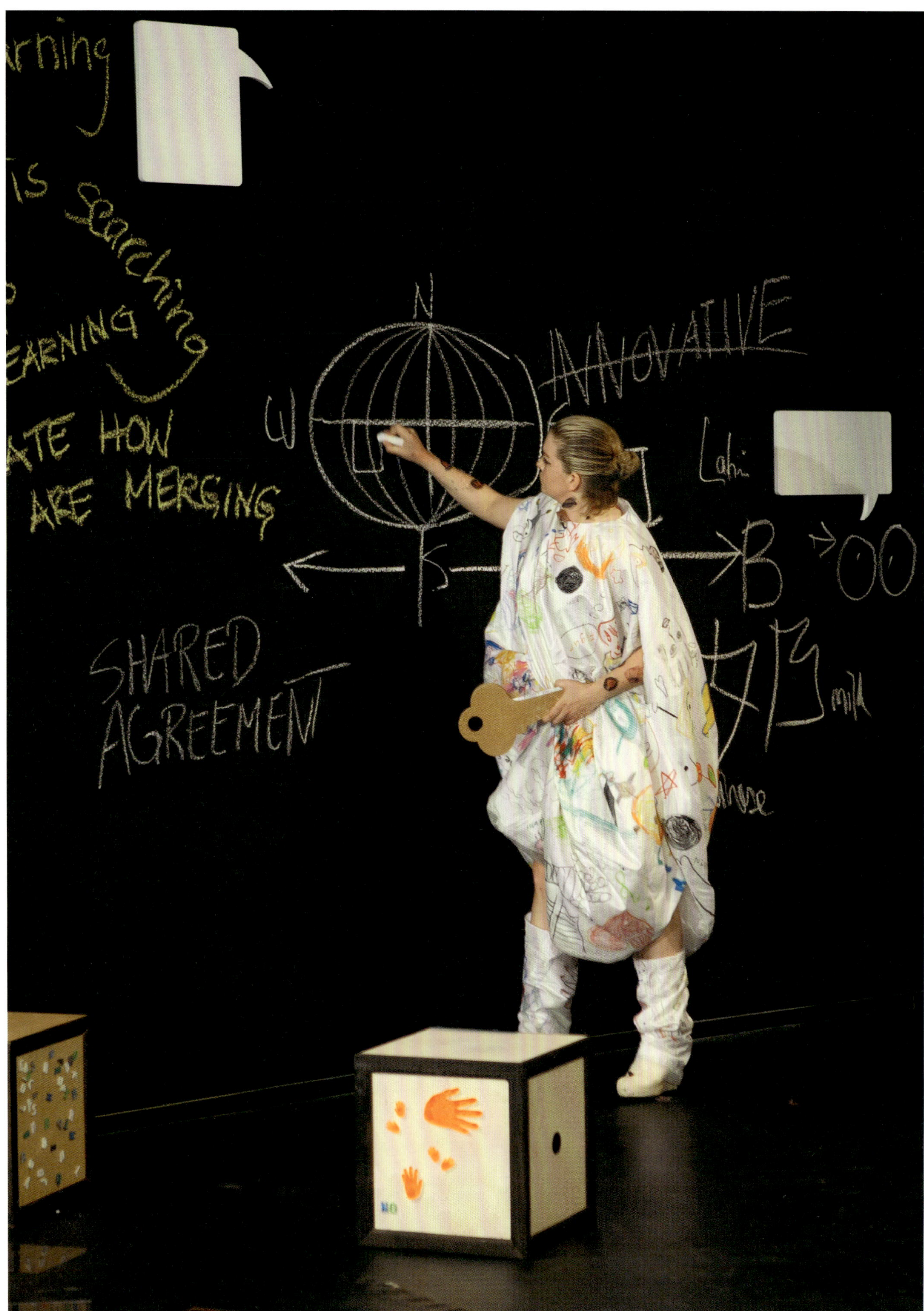
searching
N
W
S
INNOVATIVE
ARE MERGING
SHARED
AGREEMENT

Im Hinblick auf dieses große Thema unternimmt Danz den ernsthaften Versuch, eine offene und freie Atmosphäre zu schaffen, die ihren Standpunkt in ihren Songs spürbar werden lässt. Der Aufbau ihrer performativen Arbeiten beginnt – wie eine Sammlung von Gedanken, die unser Verständnis von Welt als Konstruktion bestätigt – mit der kollektiven Deutung mündlich überlieferter Geschichten. „Manche sagen, die Bücher in der Brust hätten zu sprechen begonnen", zitiert Danz ein Sprichwort der Maya. „Die Gesellschaft, nicht die Schrift bestimmt, wer wie lesen kann."

Danz setzt sich bereits seit ihrem Kunststudium mit Performance auseinander. Damals entwarf sie verschiedene Szenarien, bei denen sie ihre Kostüme als förmlich lebendige Landkarten einsetzte. Ganz ähnlich funktionierten auch „Kaffeehausbilder" aus dem Nahen Osten: Wandernde Künstler zogen hierbei von Café zu Café und schilderten die Geschichte der Region mittels der in einem Gemälde dargestellten Taten und Untaten ihrer Helden und Schurken. Anstelle von Historienbildern auf Leinwand druckt Mariechen Danz ihre Motive allerdings auf eine Art Baumwollanzug, der als Bildträger sowie als Gefäß für verschlüsselte Botschaften – vielleicht über die Zukunft der Menschheit – fungiert. Als bewachten sie den Würfel und die Bühne, stehen die beiden riesigen Anzüge mit dem Titel *Common Carrier Case (Präparat)* stoisch eingezwängt zwischen zwei Glasscheiben, die von surrealistisch anmutenden Hand- und Armabgüssen aus grünem und rotem Epoxidharz zusammengehalten werden. Bei diesen als Kostüme fungierenden Skulpturen handelt es sich gleichzeitig um Digitaldrucke von Danz' Zeichnungen auf Stoff, der ausgestopft eine stabile, aufrechte Haltung gewährleistet, was ihm das atavistische Aussehen geharnischter Samurai verleiht. Auf der Vorderseite begegnen uns erneut die allgegenwärtigen Bilder von Eingeweiden, Gehirnen oder Rückenmark, die wie Pflanzen miteinander verschmelzen. Auf der Rückseite finden sich Frottagen von Münzporträts, der Kopf des Homo erectus und andere biofigurative Gebilde. Danz schlägt avatarhafte Modelle vor, die das Wissen der Welt wie eine Haut tragen, mit der sie sich vor unerwarteten Angriffen schützen. Diese mit ornamenthaften, anatomischen Darstellungen versehenen und doch körperlosen Kostüme sind ein Hybrid aus frühen japanischen Mangas beziehungsweise aktuellen Animé-Produktionen und Studien physiognomischer Anomalien, die erstmals in der Antike entstanden und zu so berühmten Gelehrten des 18. Jahrhunderts wie Johann Caspar Lavater führen.

Left, pages 63–67: *Rhyme and Reason* (performance stills), 2012.

For the most part the aesthetic choices that code the varied subjects inhabiting *Cube Cell Stage* are not rarefied, but components of an accessible fundus of images—a common visual vocabulary. However, what is entirely created is Danz' theater, a fusion across the time and space continuum, where the agrarian worker coexists with the yet-to-become astral soldier communicating in a rational language threatening to slide into irrationality. Danz' questions on the hierarchy of forms and messages in a world propelled by market systems, the haves and the have-nots of information control, are ones that try to pry open a space for alternatives. It is a dialectical push and pull, a desire for differences, while simultaneously leveling the playing field. And all this is achieved with the full force of Danz' formidable convictions.

1 "How do we internalize a library," extract from *Rhyme and Reason*, Performance on 24 May 2012, GAK Gesellschaft für Aktuelle Kunst Bremen.
2 *Rhyme and Reason*, 2012.
3 *Chalk*, UNMAP 2011, see here p. 68.
4 Extract from *Rhyme and Reason*, 2012.
5 *Take Over*, UNMAP 2013, see here p. 70.

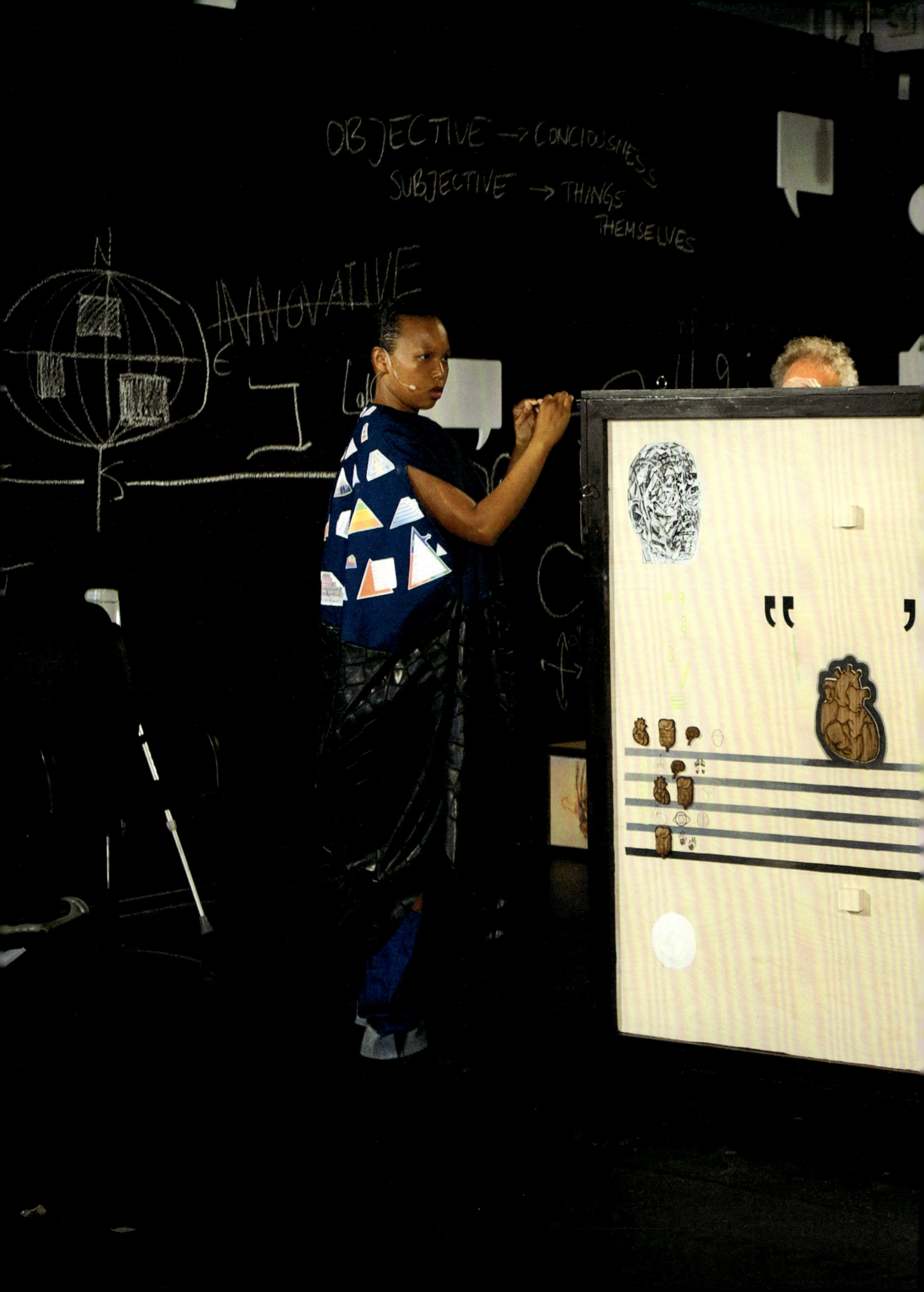
OBJECTIVE → CONCIOUSNESS
SUBJECTIVE → THINGS THEMSELVES
INNOVATIVE

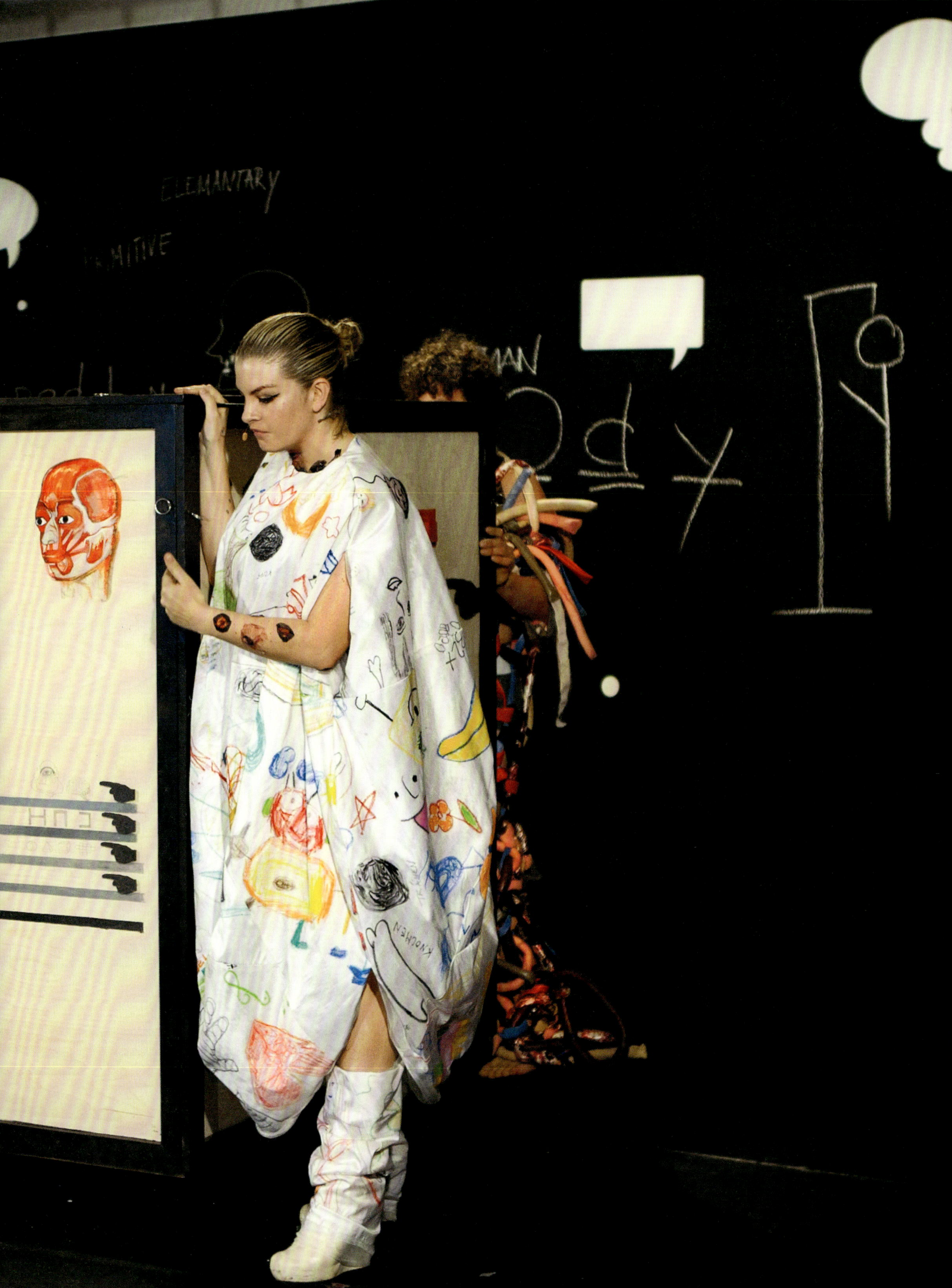
ELEMANTARY

Größtenteils sind die ästhetischen Entscheidungen, die zur Kodierung der unterschiedlichen Themen von *Cube Cell Stage* führen, keinesfalls außergewöhnlich, sondern vielmehr Bestandteile eines frei zugänglichen Bilderfundus – eines allgemeinen visuellen Vokabulars. Völlig frei erfunden hingegen ist Danz' Theater, eine über das Raum-Zeit-Kontinuum hinausgehende Verschmelzung, bei der der Landarbeiter neben dem heute noch unbekannten Weltraumsoldaten existiert und sich mit ihm in einer rationalen Sprache verständigt, die ins Irrationale abzugleiten droht. Danz' Fragen zur Hierarchie von Formen und Aussagen sollen angesichts einer Welt, die von marktwirtschaftlichen Systemen und über die Informationskontrolle Verfügenden (beziehungsweise nicht Verfügenden) beherrscht wird, einen Raum für Alternativen schaffen. Es geht hierbei um dialektische Anziehungs- und Abstoßungskräfte, um ein Bedürfnis nach Differenzen bei gleichzeitiger Nivellierung des Spielfeldes. All das erreicht Mariechen Danz aufgrund der enormen Wirkung ihrer Überzeugung, die in allen Erscheinungsformen ihres künstlerischen Schaffens zum Ausdruck kommt.

1 „How do we internalize a library?“, heißt es in der Performance *Rhyme and Reason*, aufgeführt am 24. Mai 2012 in der GAK Gesellschaft für Aktuelle Kunst Bremen.
2 *Rhyme and Reason*, 2012.
3 *Chalk*, UNMAP 2011, s. hier S. 68.
4 Zitat aus *Rhyme and Reason*, 2012.
5 *Take Over*, UNMAP 2013, s. hier S. 70.

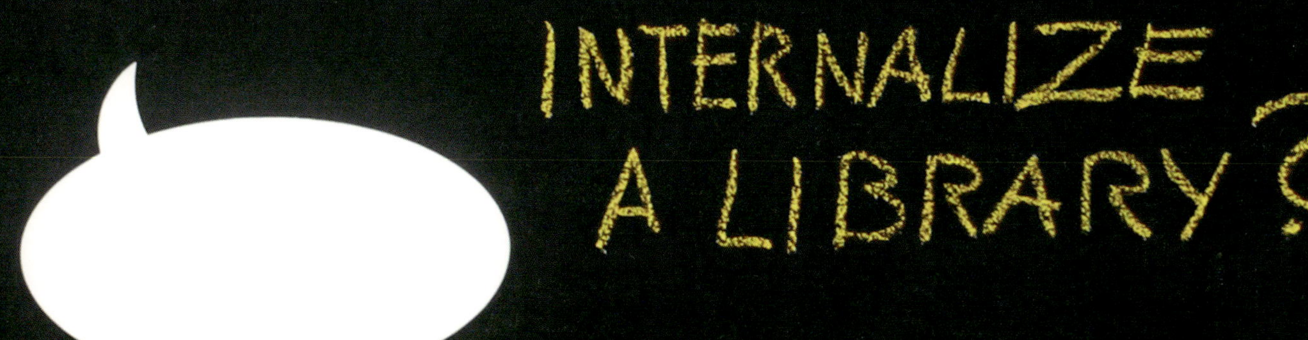

MEMORY IS NOT INTELLIGENCE.
TO REPEAT IS NOT TO KNOW
COMPARISON ISN'T REASON.
THERE IS THE GROUND
AND THE BACKGROUND
KNOWLEDGE IS NOT JUST
LINEAR MIMICRY

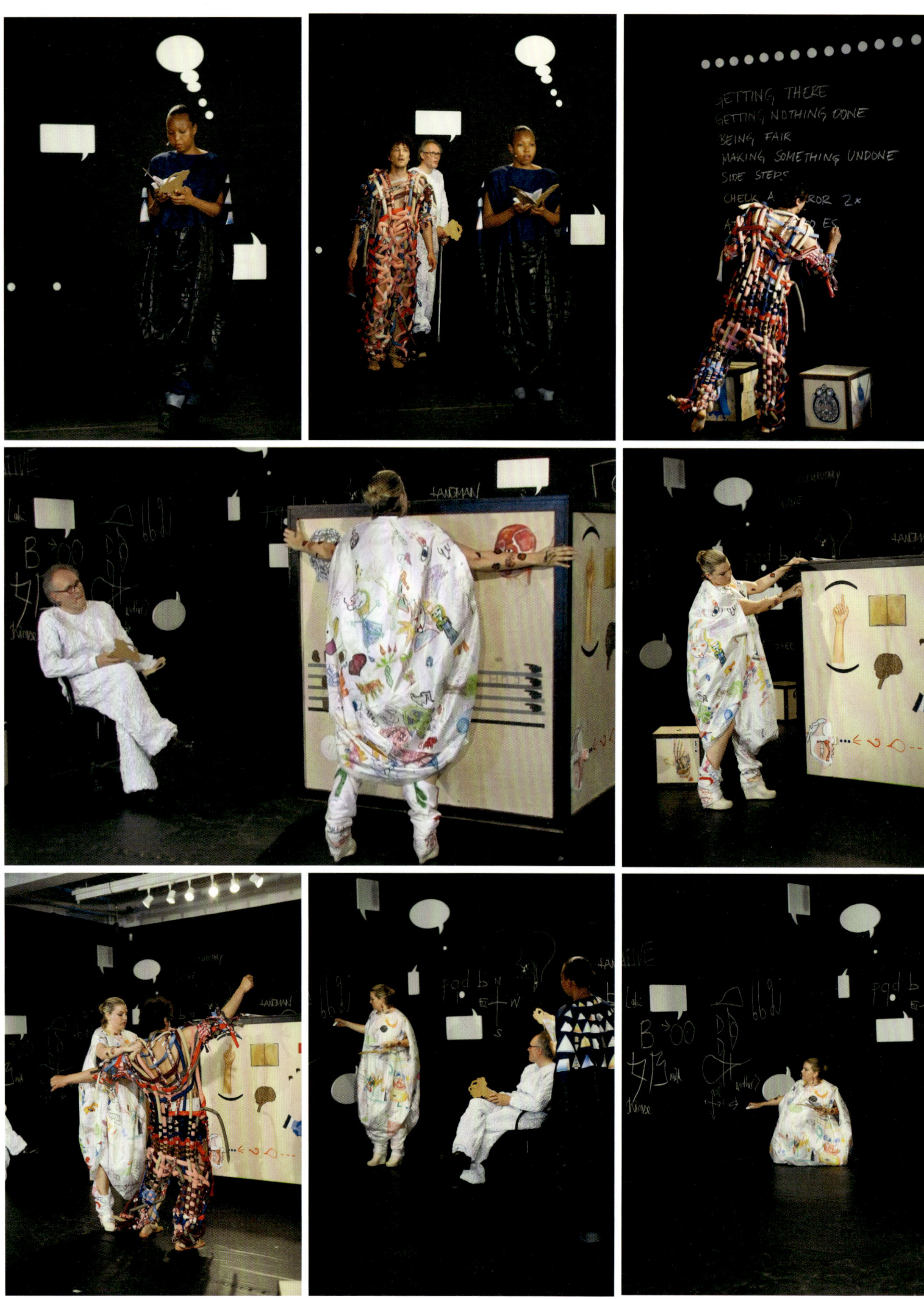
GETTING THERE
GETTING NOTHING DONE
BEING FAIR
MAKING SOMETHING UNDONE

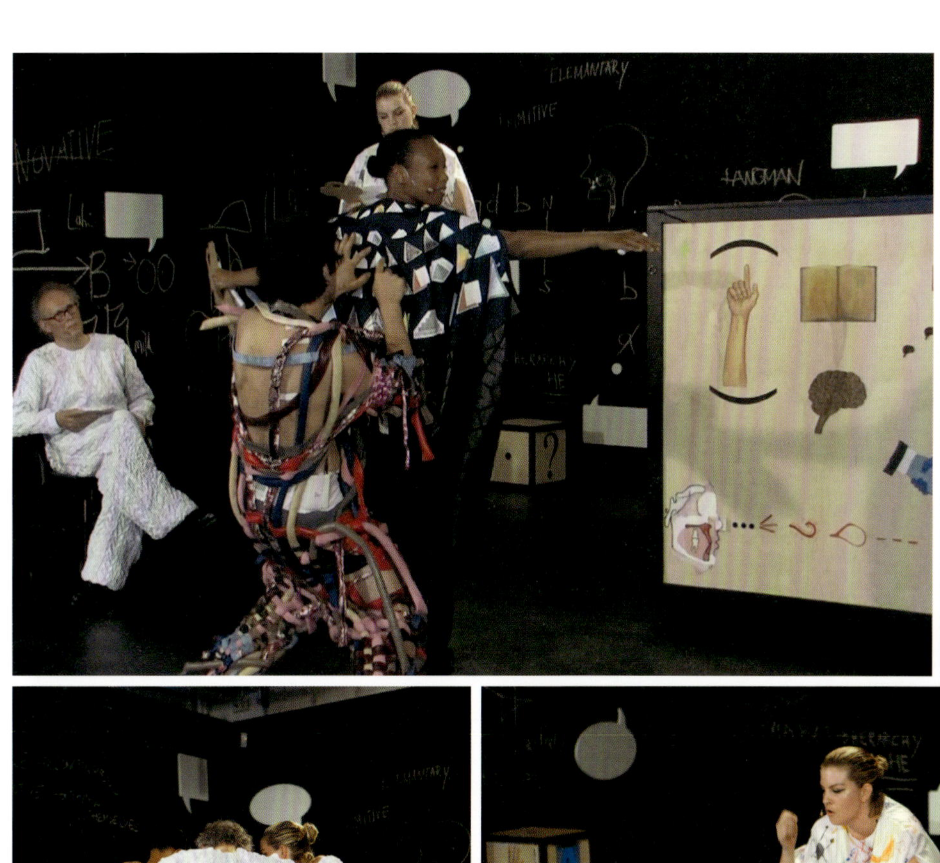
ELEMANTARY
HANGMAN

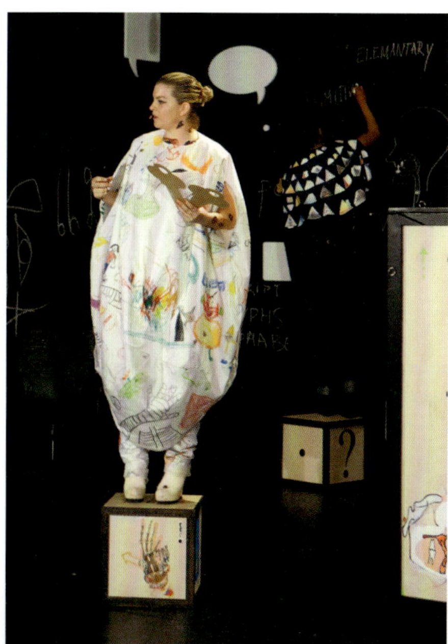

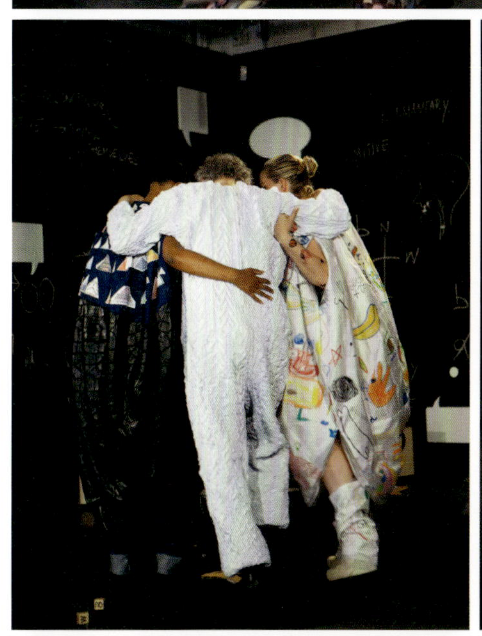

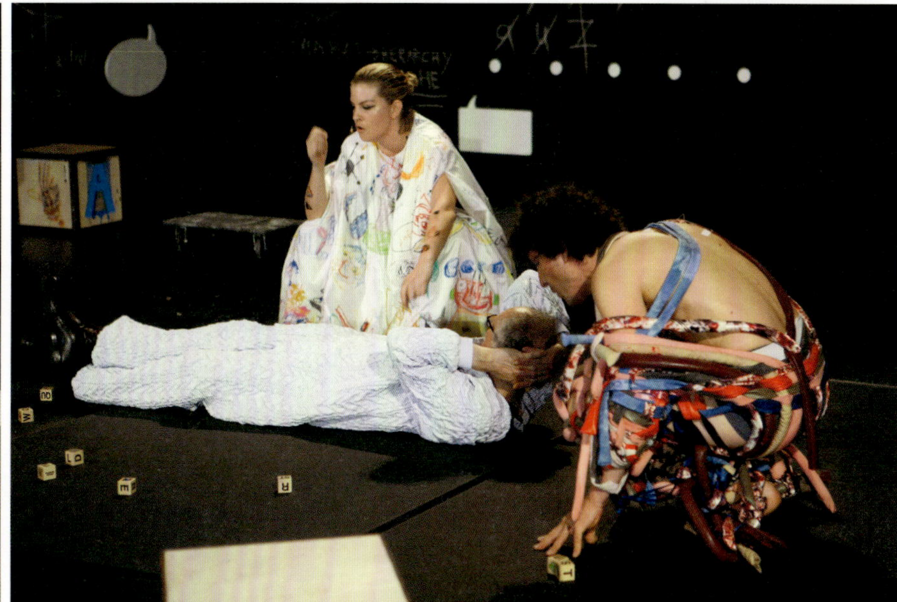

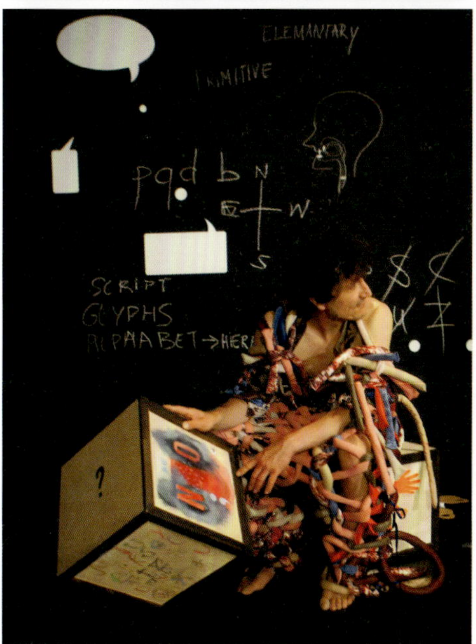
ELEMANTARY
SCRIPT
GLYPHS

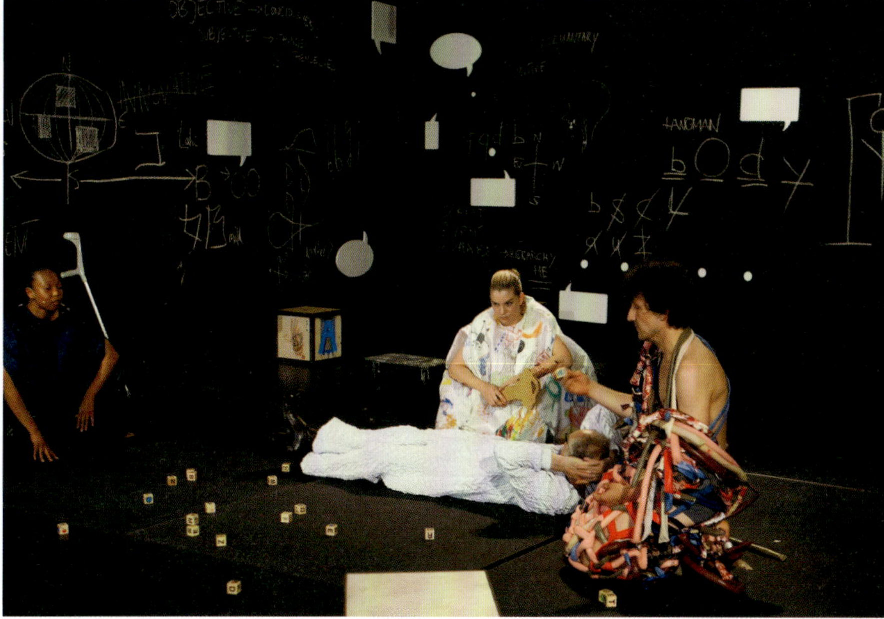
HANGMAN
body

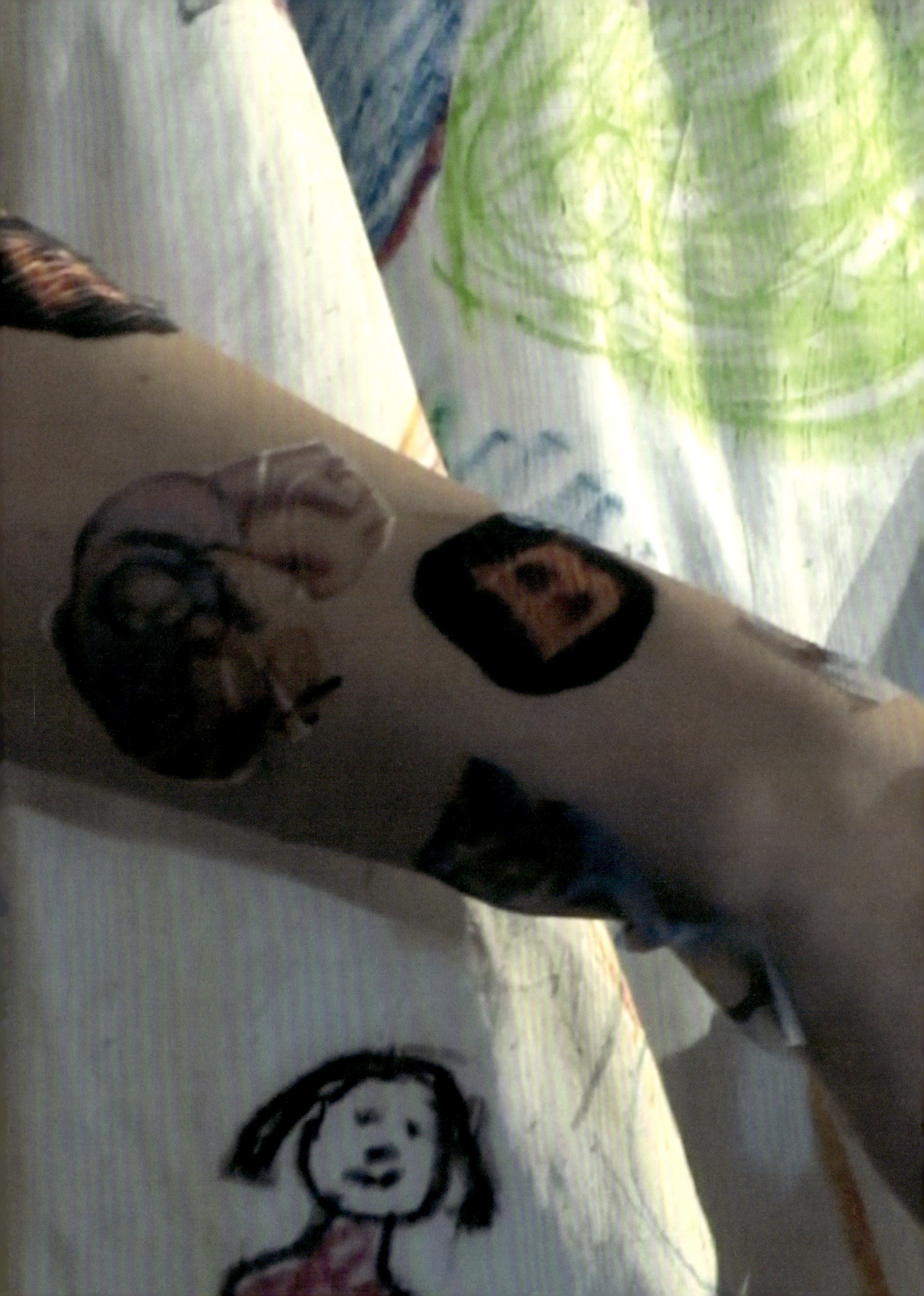

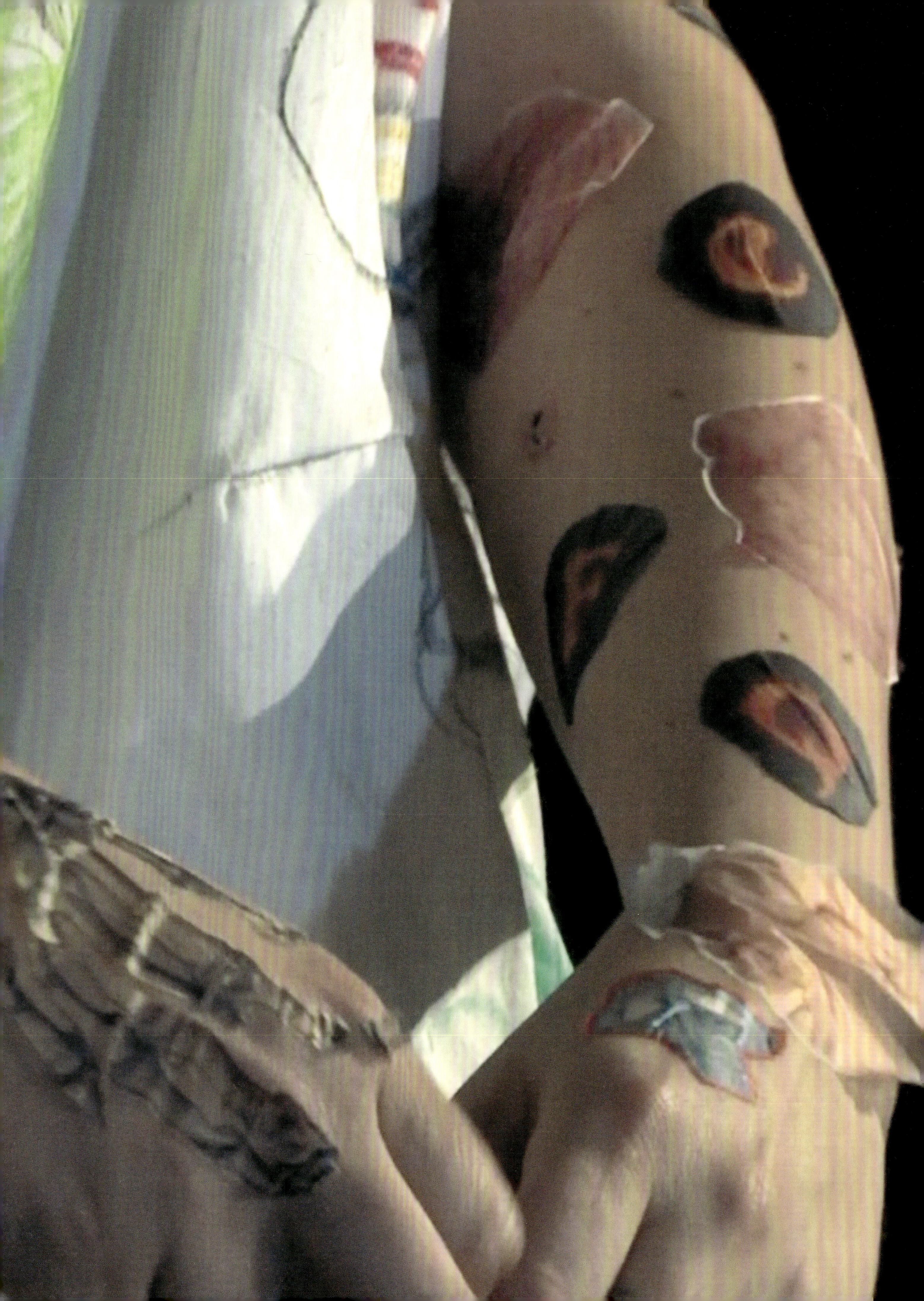

CHALK

Lyrics: Mariechen Danz
Music: UNMAP

Download Link für / for CHALK:
http://smarturl.it/unmap-chalk

WRITE A WORD
A MARK, A LEARNING
TO ILLUSTRATE HOW
LANGUAGE IS SEARCHING
POINT ON MAP
A MARK, A LEARNING
TO RELOCATE WHERE
BORDERS ARE MERGING
AND WHOS NURSING?
OR OPERATING?

NO MEMORY, NO LEARNING, A KEY

INFORMATION
ACQUISITION
PROCESS PRODUCT
ENDLESS CHURNING
EDUCATION
IN RELATION
COUNTING DOWN THIS
THIS YEARLY EARNING
WHAT TO GAIN FROM
NAME A RUMOR
LIKE A FEVER
HOLDS A TUMOR
MY HEART RACES
BATTLES, PACES
LANDING LINE
VEINS OF THE NATIONS

NO MEMORY, NO LEARNING
ORGAN INPUT, OUTPUT SYSTEM

BLUEPRINT FOR
A REGULATION
REITERATE THAT:
ORGANS CORRESPOND TO
SOCIAL STRUCTURES?
OR RULING PRESSURES?
NO MEMORY, NO LEARNING, A KEY

NO MEMORY, NO LEARNING
ORGAN INPUT, OUTPUT SYSTEM

TAKE OVER

Lyrics: Mariechen Danz
Music: UNMAP
[1] Inspired by: Guillermo Gomez Pena

GETTING THERE, GETTING NOTHING DONE
BEING FAIR, MAKING SOMETHING UNDONE
SIDESTEPS: CHECK AN ERROR, CHECK AN ERROR
ATTEMPTING TO ESTABLISH
SOME BASIC CONNECTION
I WISH I HAD A CHANGE OF PACE
IN ORDER TO TRACE WHERE
ALL TROUBLE COMES FROM
MIGRATING IN REVERSE
BACK TO THE ORIGINS
SIDESTEPPING IN REVERSE
NOW THAT I FOUND YOU
NOW THAT I LET YOU GO
TAKE IT TO THE ROAD AND RUN
LOOKING FOR YOUR FACE TO SHOW

GETTING THERE, GETTING NOTHING DONE
BEING FAIR, MAKING SOMETHING UNDONE
SPELL-CHECK: MAKE AN ERROR
LIKE IT´S AN ADVANTAGE
NO MAPS AND NO LANGUAGE
WISH I COULD NAME THE FACE
TO UNDERSTAND OR TRACE WHERE
ALL TROUBLE COMES FROM
MIGRATING IN REVERSE
BACK TO THE ORIGINS
SIDESTEPPING IN REVERSE
NOW THAT I FOUND YOU
NOW THAT I LET YOU GO
TAKE IT TO THE ROAD AND RUN
LOOKING FOR YOUR FACE TO SHOW

"EXCUSE ME SIR:
CAN YOU SPEAK TO ME IN A LANGUAGE
I DON'T UNDERSTAND, NO BIG DEAL
IT'S JUST THAT I'M OBSESSED WITH
ATTEMPTING TO ESTABLISH
SOME BASIC CONNECTION
BETWEEN BODY, HISTORY, DESTINY
POLITICS OF LANGUAGE
& PSYCHOLOGY
IS NO WAY TO ESTABLISH
SOME BASIC CONNECTION
OH WAIT I HAD A CHANGE OF PACE
AND 'TAKE-OVER'
WHERE ALL THE TROUBLE COMES FROM
MIGRATING IN REVERSE
BACK TO THE ORIGINS
HE SAID: 'HE WAS FIRST!'" [1]

WHERE ALL THE TROUBLE
COMES FROM

WERKLISTE / LIST OF WORKS

(in chronologischer Reihenfolge /
in chronological order)

Hold Armor I (map), 2007–2010
Graphit, Farbstifte auf Papier /
Graphite, colored pencil on paper,
180 x 96 cm

Hold Armor II (map), 2007–2010
Graphit, Farbstifte auf Papier /
Graphite, colored pencil on paper
178,5 x 108 cm

Pressure (map), 2010
Graphit auf Papier /
Graphite on paper
236 x 110 cm

Common Carrier Case 1, 2011
Graphit auf Papier /
Graphite on paper
137,2 x 130 cm

Common Carrier Case 1 (Präparat), 2011
Digitalprint auf Baumwolle, Watte, Plexiglas, Epoxid /
Digital print on cotton, wadding, Plexiglas, epoxy
177,4 x 153 x 51 cm

Soil Sample Organ (Bone), 2011
Polyurethan, Zweige /
Polyurethane, twigs
10 x 5 x 44 cm

Common Carrier Case 2 (Avatar), 2012
Graphit auf Papier /
Graphite on paper
137,2 x 130 cm

Common Carrier Case 2 (Präparat – Avatar), 2012
Digitalprint auf Baumwolle, Watte, Plexiglas, Epoxid /
Digital print on cotton, wadding, Plexiglas, epoxy
177,4 x 153 x 51 cm

Book (unlearning) 1, 2012
Polyurethan, Aluminium, Kupfer /
Polyurethane, aluminium, copper
30 x 40 cm

Learning Organ (intestine), 2012
Polyurethan, Ton /
Polyurethane, modeling clay
32,5 x 23 cm

Learning Cubes TV Tower, 2012
Mixed Media-Installation /
Mixed media installation
Größe variabel / Dimensions variable
Beinhaltet / Includes:

Complain the Explanation, 2008
Performance-Dokumentation / Performance documentation, California Institute for the Arts
15:15 min.
Video: Alina Skrzeszewska, Carlin Wing
Akteur/innen / Participants: Erek Daves, Achraf El-Bahi, Jackson Fledermaus, Aimee Goguen, Julie Mattei, Matt Siegle, Breanna Sinclaire

un un learning, 2011
HD-Video, Farbe / Color, Ton / Sound
19:06 min.
Video: Andrea Huyoff, Alina Skrzeszewska
Ton / Sound: StudioMueller.de

Knot in Arrow: The Dig of No Body, 2011
Performance-Dokumentation / Performance documentation, *Based in Berlin*, Berlin
15:10 min.
Akteur/innen / Participants: Mariechen Danz, Ronel Doual, Matthias Geserick, Alex Stolze
Video: Andrea Huyoff, Stine Marie Jacobsen, Alina Skrzeszewska
Ton / Sound: StudioMueller.de

Rhyme and Reason, Performance 24. Mai 2012 / May 24, 2012, GAK Gesellschaft für Aktuelle Kunst Bremen:
Akteur/innen / Participants: Mariechen Danz,
Ronel Doual, Wolfgang Hainke, Alex Stolze
Kamera / Camera: Andrea Huyoff, Stine Marie Jacobsen
Ton / Sound: Florian Wilke
Postproduktion / Postproduction: Schnitt / Cut: Dani Gal,
Farbkorrektur / Color correction: Sebastian Bodirsky,
Ton / Sound: Christian Obermaier

Giant Learning Cube, seit/since 2012
Holz, Acryl, Plexiglas, Tafellack (innen)
Der Kubus lässt sich zu einer 6 Meter-Bühne ausklappen.
Kubus: 150 x 150 x 150 cm, Bühne 600 x 450 x 150 cm
Wood, acrylic, Plexiglas, black chalk board paint (inside)
Cube unfolds into a 6 meter stage.
Cubus: 150 x 150 x 150 cm, Stage: 600 x 450 x 150 cm

Body/ydob, a flayed mirage, 2012
Stoffmalkreide auf Seide, Kupfer / Crayon on silk, copper
Zeichnungen: Nashorn-Schüler, Bremen /
Drawings: Rhino pupils, Bremen
Größe variabel / Dimensions variable

Alle Arbeiten / All works:
Courtesy die Künstlerin / the artist und / and
Galerie Tanja Wagner, Berlin.

BIOGRAFIE / BIOGRAPHY

geboren / born 1980 in Dublin
lebt / lives in Berlin

AUSBILDUNG / EDUCATION

2008 MFA in Art & Integrated Media, California Institute of the Arts, Valencia
2005 Meisterschülerin / Master class student, Universität der Künste, Berlin (Klasse / class Leiko Ikemura)
2003 Audio-Visual Media, Gerrit Rietveld Academy, Amsterdam
1999 Certificate in Art & Design, Sallynoggin College, Dublin

PREISE UND STIPENDIEN / SCHOLARSHIPS AND AWARDS

2013 Villa Romana-Preis, Florenz / Florence
2006–08 CalArts Interdisciplinary Grant
2002–05 Cusanuswerk

Rhyme and Reason (detail), 2012.

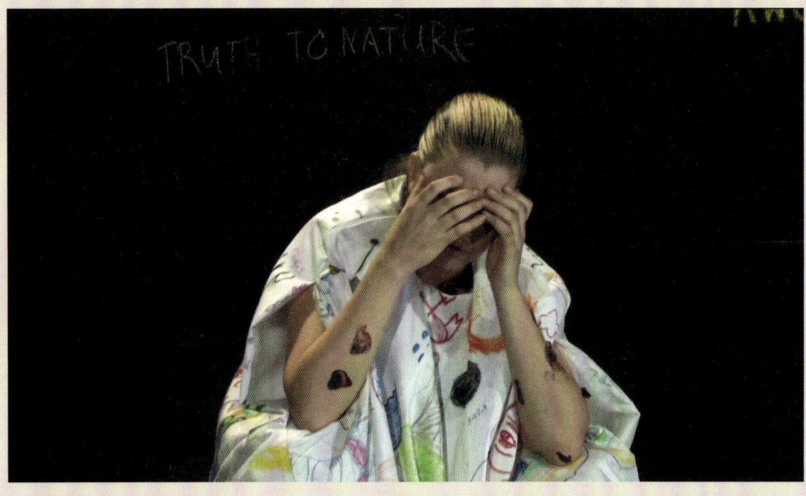

EINZELAUSSTELLUNGEN UND PERFORMANCES / SOLO EXHIBITIONS AND PERFORMANCES (AUSWAHL / SELECTION)

2013 Album *Pressures,* UNMAP (Mariechen Danz, Thomas Fietz, Matthias Geserick, Alexander Stolze), Sinnbus Berlin
Imprint Pressures, Galerie Tanja Wagner, Berlin
Ink Set., Venus & Apoll, Julia Stoschek Collection, Düsseldorf / Dusseldorf
‚Statue for Gesticulation' – ein Lied (Performance), Kunsthaus Bregenz
2012 *CUBE CELL STAGE,* Kunstverein Göttingen
Rhyme and Reason (Performance), GAK Gesellschaft für Aktuelle Kunst Bremen
CUBE CELL STAGE, GAK Gesellschaft für Aktuelle Kunst, Bremen
2011 *KNOW AEON, KNOW OMIT,* Galerie Tanja Wagner, Berlin
The Dig of No Body (Performance), *Based in Berlin*, Atelierhaus Monbijoupark, Berlin
2010 *Mapping the subaltern: an ideographic balance* (mit / with Alvaro Guillen), Koh-i-noor Projects, Kopenhagen / Copenhagen
Art Forum Berlin, Galerie Tanja Wagner, Berlin
Tower Vessel Tooth, TÄT Projects, Berlin
2009 *They Cast No Shadow* (mit / with Daniel Fabian), Gallery 1927, Los Angeles
Complain the Explanation (Performance), New Museum, New York
Fist: emoting structures (Performance), 10th OPEN International Performance Art Festival, Peking / Beijing

2008 *Mapping the subaltern: a subjective geography* (Performance mit / with Alvaro Guillen), Wight Biennial, Broad Art Center, Los Angeles
Complain the Explanation (Performance), Peres Projects & other locations, Los Angeles
Complain the Explanation (Performance), gallery d301 CalArts, Valencia
Fossilizing the Body Border Disorder – a Diorama, gallery d301CalArts, Valencia
Wolf (Performance), Wildness at Silverplatter, Los Angeles
2007 *Gospel of Bully* (Performance), Kasseler KunstVerein
2005 *Heartattack* (Performance), Areal 28 Projects, Berlin
Solas-Un (Performance), Kunsthaus Potsdam
Solas-Un (Performance), Universität der Künste, Berlin
Marsmother (Performance mit / with Leiko Ikemura), Kunststation Sankt Peter, Köln / Cologne

GRUPPENAUSSTELLUNGEN / GROUP EXHIBITIONS (AUSWAHL / SELECTION)

2013 *Villa Romana 1905–2013*, Bundeskunsthalle, Bonn
Süden – Villa Romana in Berlin, Deutsche Bank KunstHalle, Berlin
Nouvelles Vagues / A History of Inspiration, Palais de Tokyo, Paris
CULM, Night Gallery, Los Angeles
Berlin.Status 02, Künstlerhaus Bethanien, Berlin
Liebe ist kälter als das Kapital, Kunsthaus Bregenz
2012 *Discussing Metamodernism*, Galerie Tanja Wagner, Berlin
30 Künstler – 30 Räume, Institut für moderne Kunst, Nürnberg / Nuremberg
2011 *No more Modern: Notes on Metamodernism*, The Museum of Art and Design, New York
4th Moscow Biennale of Contemporary Art
863 km, Scheubein Fine Art, Zürich / Zurich
Based in Berlin, Atelierhaus Monbijoupark, Berlin
HotSpot Berlin 2011, Georg-Kolbe-Museum, Berlin
2010 *Die Tür geht nach Innen auf*, Galerie Tanja Wagner, Berlin
Ein Fest Für Boris Akt II, Galerie Vittorio Manalese, Berlin
Get Behind Me Satan and Push, Peres Projects, Berlin
Volume, AT1 Projects, Los Angeles
Ins Blickfeld gerückt, Institut Français, Berlin
Aka Symbol, organisiert von / organized by Mariechen Danz, HBC und / and Forgotten Bar Project, Berlin
2009 *Zeigen. Eine Audiotour durch Berlin von Karin Sander*, Temporäre Kunsthalle Berlin
Younger than Jesus, New Museum, New York
Building Paradise (mit / with Liz Glynn), 7th & Fig art space, Los Angeles
2008 *Of Men For Men By Women*, Forgotten Bar Project, Berlin
Freude der Jugend III, Artnews Projects, Berlin
We want a New Object, Peres Projects & other locations (Chinatown, Los Angeles, CalArts grad show)
The Graduation, Veslavsky Panorama, Los Angeles
2007 *Animal Style*, 29025 Eveningside Dr Exhibition, Val Verde
It could all be so simple but I'd rather make it hard, MFA Mid-Res Exhibition, CalArts, Valencia
Leiko Ikemura und ihre Meisterschüler, Kunstverein Baden-Baden
12 Artists from Germany, Dangerous Curve Gallery, Los Angeles
Exquisite Acts & Everyday Rebellions, CalArts, Valencia
2006 *Lieber Friedrich*, Kasseler Kunstverein
2005 *Muse Heute*, Kunsthalle Bremen
Spielraum, Kunstverein Potsdam
2003 *Peepshow*, Arti et Amicatae, Amsterdam
2002 *Trilemma*, Kunstverein Potsdam
2001 *Zwischen Tür und Angel*, Zionskirche, Berlin
Die Vertreibung der Händler aus dem Tempel, Gallery 2YK, Berlin

Dieser Katalog erscheint anlässlich der Ausstellungen /
This catalogue has been published on the occasion of the exhibitions

MARIECHEN DANZ. CUBE CELL STAGE

10. März – 3. Juni 2012 / March 10 – June 3, 2012
GAK Gesellschaft für Aktuelle Kunst Bremen und / and
17. Juni – 29. Juli 2012 / June 17 – July 29, 2012, Kunstverein Göttingen

GAK GESELLSCHAFT FÜR AKTUELLE KUNST

Teerhof 21, D-28199 Bremen, T. +49 (0)421 500897
F. +49 (0)421 593337, office@gak-bremen.de
www.gak-bremen.de

Direktorin / Director: Janneke de Vries
Vorstand / Board Members: David Bartusch (1. Vorsitzender / Chief of the board), Daniel de Olano (stellvertr. Vorsitzender / Vice chairman), Dr. Joachim Kreibohm (stellvertr. Vorsitzender / Vice chairman), Dieter Eckert (Schatzmeister / Treasurer), Marion Bertram (Schriftführerin / Secretary)

Ausstellung / Exhibition:
Kuratorin / Curator: Janneke de Vries
Kuratorische Assistenz / Assistant Curator: Yvonne Bialek
Koordination / Coordinator: Svea Kellner
Aufbau / Installation: Katja Blum, Conor Gilligan, Markus Oldenburg, Z. Schmidt, Thorsten Wieckert, Florian Wilke
Praktikum / Internship: Victoria Ruhe, Carmen Rodriguez Godino
Wochenendaufsicht / Weekend's Custody: Susanne Bollenhagen, Kathrin Schaffhäuser

KUNSTVEREIN GÖTTINGEN

Gotmar Straße 1 / D-37073 Göttingen, T. +49 (0)551 44899
www.kunstvereingoettingen.de, info@kunstvereingoettingen.de

Künstlerische Leitung / Artistic Director: Laura Schleussner
Geschäftsführer / Business Manager: Helmut Wenzel

Vorstand / Board Members: Laura Schleussner (1. Vorsitzende / Chief of the board), Prof. Dr. Kurt von Figura (stellvertr. Vorsitzender / Vice chairman), Friedrich-Wilhelm Becker, Jürgen Beyer, Andrea Ruhstraht

KATALOG / CATALOGUE

Herausgeber / Editors: Laura Schleussner, Janneke de Vries
Redaktion / Editing: Yvonne Bialek, Svea Kellner, Janneke de Vries
Lektorat / Copy editing: Svea Kellner, Laura Schleussner, Janneke de Vries
Übersetzung / Translation: Ralf Schauff (Smith: d), Laura Schleussner (de Vries: e), Kennedy Unglaub Translations (Schleussner: d)
Fotonachweis / Photo credits: Mariechen Danz, Franziska von den Driesch, Philip Fleischer, Peter Heller, Tobias Hübel, Paula Winkler
Gestaltung / Design: Hardin Kirsch, www.hardin-kirsch.de
Produktion / Production management: DISTANZ Verlag, Sonja Bahr
Druck / Production: optimal media GmbH, Röbel/Müritz

VERTRIEB / DISTRIBUTION

Gestalten, Berlin
www.gestalten.com, sales@gestalten.com
ISBN 978-3-942405-86-7, Printed in Germany

ERSCHIENEN BEI / PUBLISHED BY

DISTANZ Verlag
www.distanz.de

Unser Dank gilt den Hauptförderern /
We would like to thank our main sponsors for their generous support:

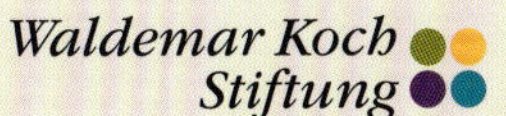

Conrad Naber Stiftung

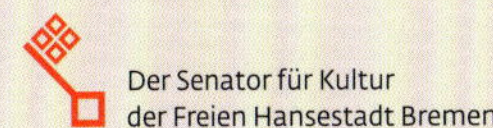

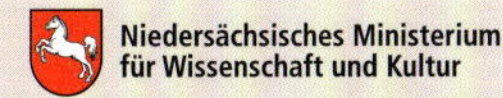

Außerdem danken wir / Furthermore we wish to thank:
Galerie Tanja Wagner, Berlin; Sculpture Berlin und / and Genghis Khan Fabrication Co.

Mariechen Danz dankt / thanks: Silva Agostini, Yvonne Bialek, Danz Family, Werner Vaudlet und den Schülern / and the pupils @ Das Nashorn, Ronel Doual, Thomas Fietz, Dani Gal, Matthias Geserick, Liz Glynn, Claudia Gonschorek, Alvaro Guillen, Wolfgang Hainke, Nina Hoffmann, Andrea Huyoff, Stine Marie Jacobsen, Rahel Keller, Svea Kellner, Hardin Kirsch, Helmut Wenzel & Anja Marrack @ Kunstverein Göttingen, Christian Maier @ Sculpture Berlin, Jennifer Schild, Laura Schleussner, Sara Schwartz, Sinnbus, Alina Skrzeszewska, Valerie Smith, Alex Stolze, Nina Tabassomi, UNMAP, Janneke de Vries, Tanja Wagner

STIFTUNGKUNSTFONDS

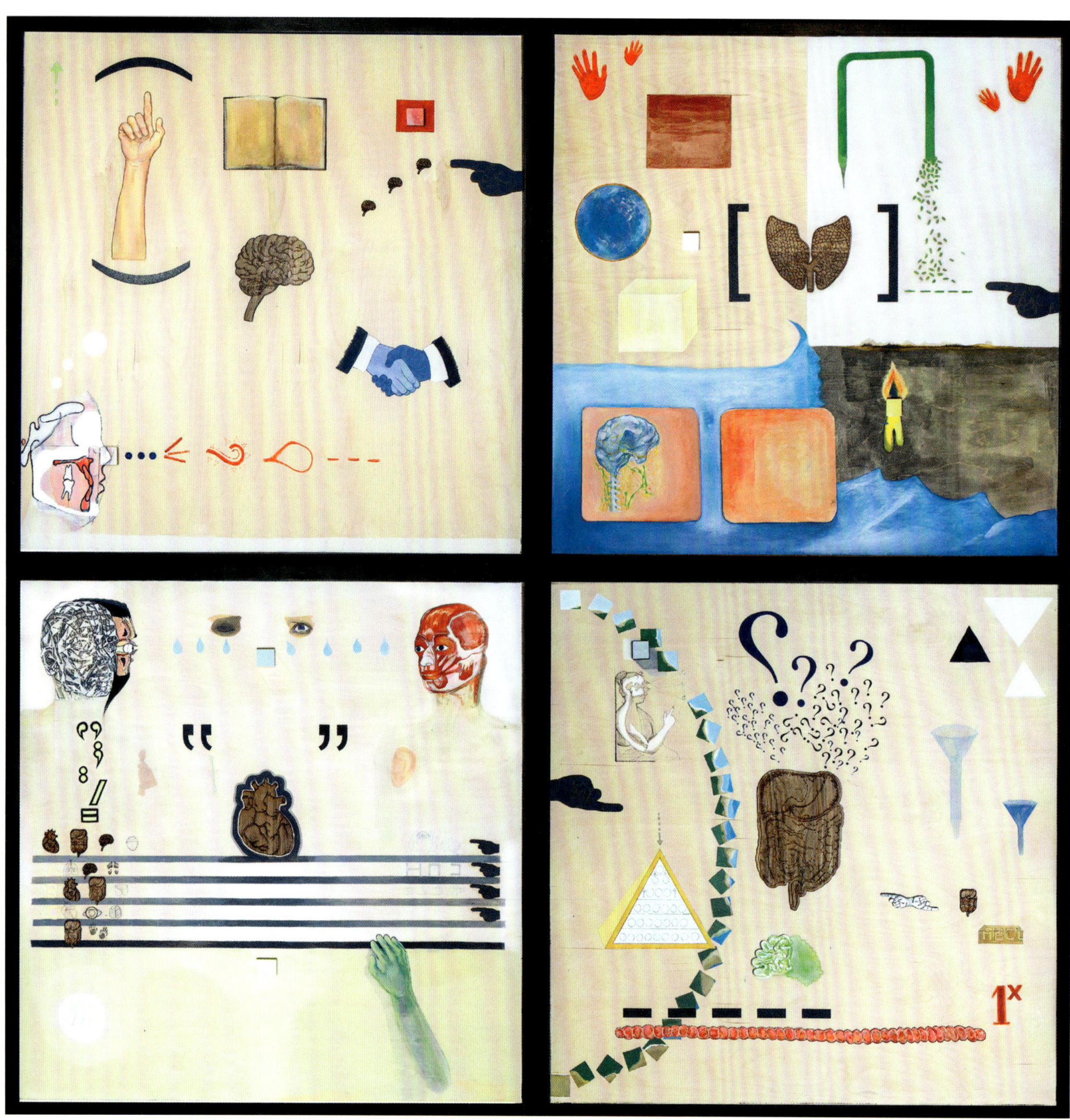

Giant Learning Cube, since 2012 (side walls).

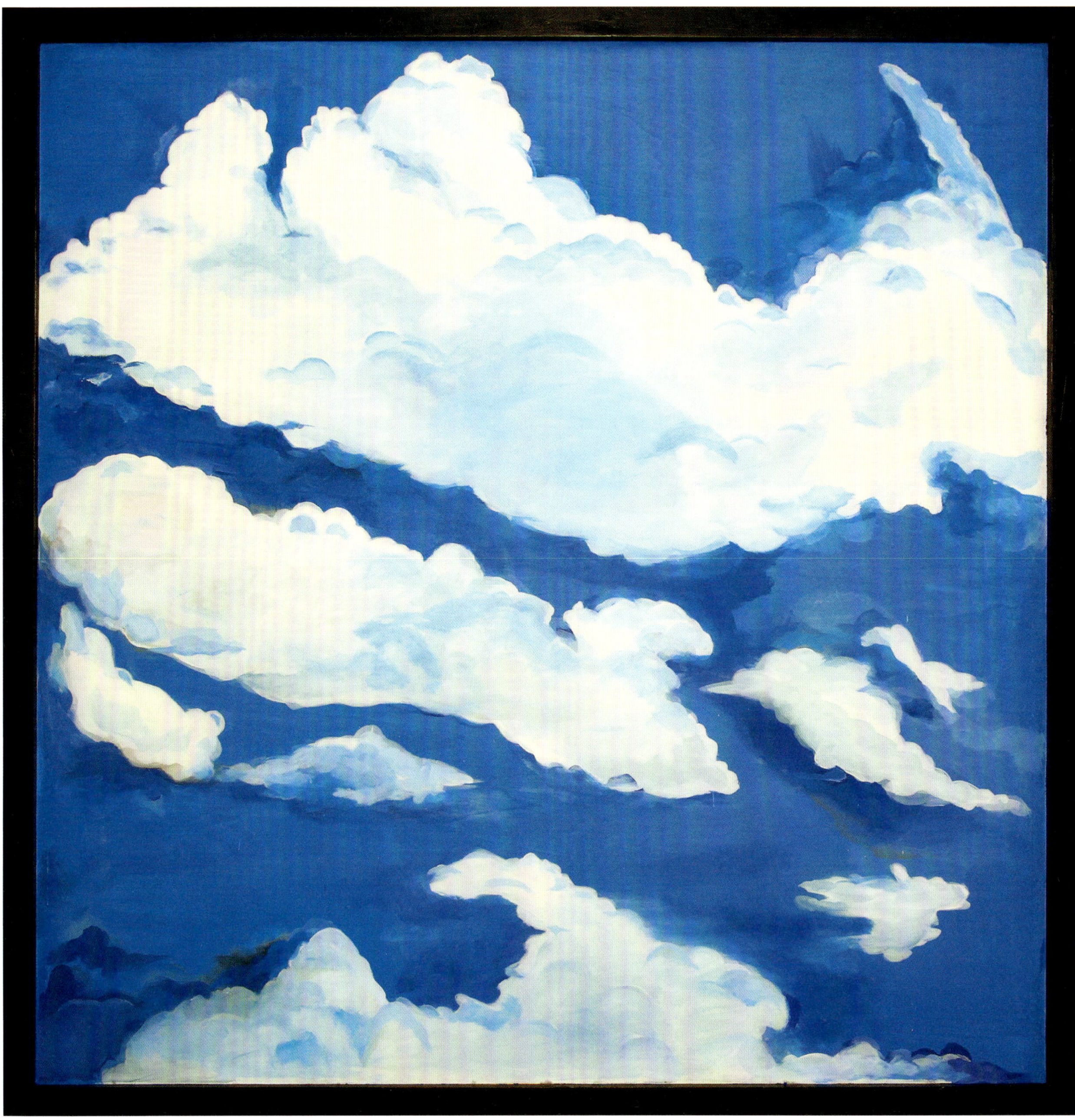

Giant Learning Cube, since 2012 (top).

Following page: Extract from Ámbar Past, *Incantations: Songs, Spells and Images by Mayan Women*, El Paso 2009.

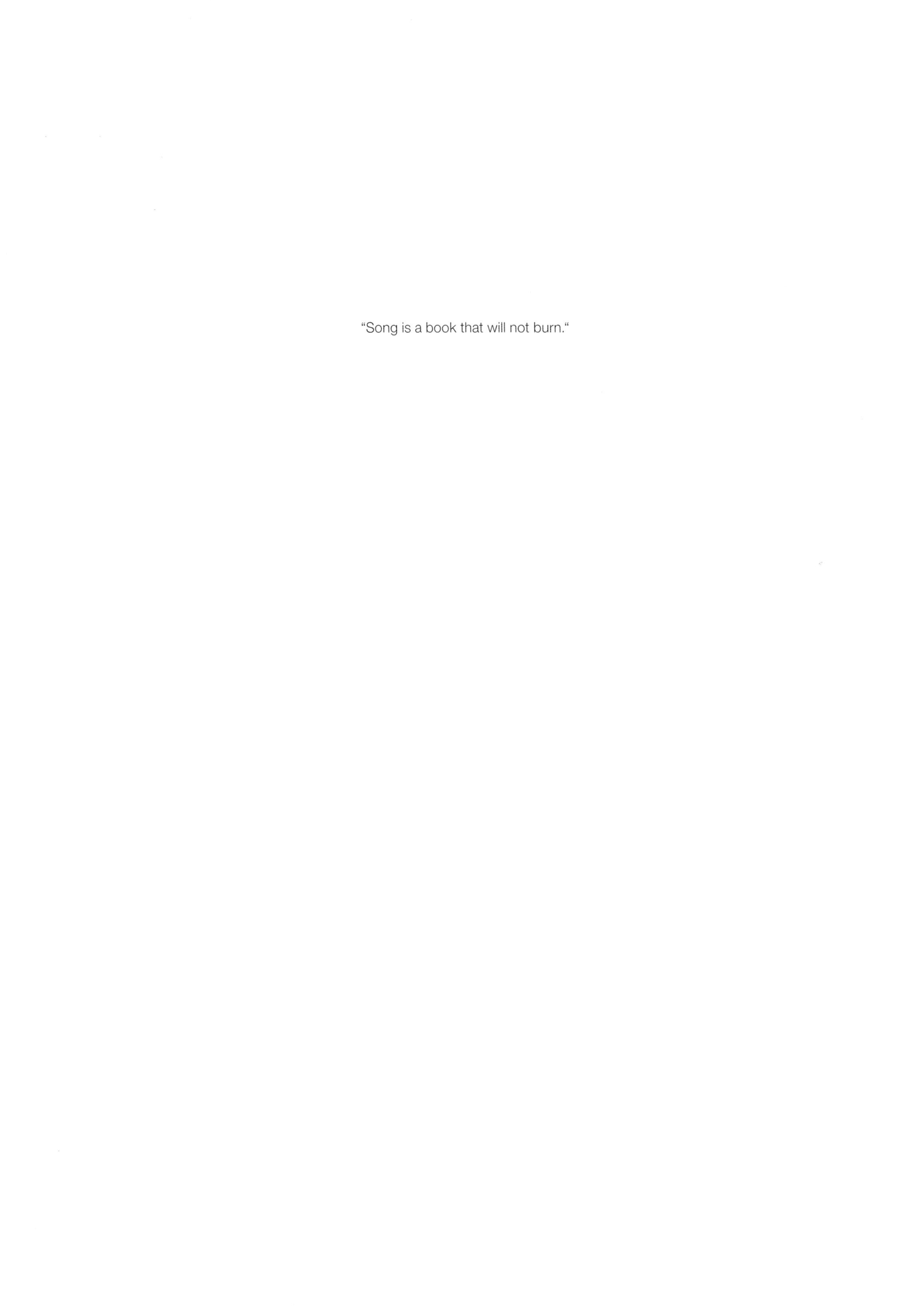

“Song is a book that will not burn.“